Ntozake
Plays. 1

for colored girls who have considered suicide/ when the rainbow is enuf, spell #7, The Love Space Demands

for colored girls... : 'Downright extraordinary. Seven women in brilliantly coloured dresses swirl through 22 dance-poems in an exposition of the "metaphysical dilemmas" of race, gender and environment ... as intelligent as it is harrowing.' *Time Out*

spell #7: 'Takes us right into the hinterland and psyche of what it means to be black and American. The structure is daring – a kaleidoscope of characters shimmer before our eyes as Shange weaves a magical tapestry of racial history – of humiliations, of gold – images tumble, cartwheel and somersault before us.' *City Limits*
'As in Shange's *for colored girls* ..., this play takes the form of eloquent monologues bristling with anger, humour and poetry ... language that longs to dance.' *Observer*

The Love Space Demands: 'What is striking about the 70-minute show is its verbal vividness and progression of mood ... Shange's biting, forceful poems seem to me not just about the gap between the sexes and the races, but about the gulf that separates middle-class angst and underprivileged despair.' *Guardian*

Ntozake Shange was born in Trenton, New Jersey and educated at Barnard College and the University of Southern California, where she received an MA in American Studies. Her choreopoem *for colored girls who have considered suicide/ when the rainbow is enuf* brought her Broadway success and international recognition. She is the author of an acclaimed adaptation of Bertolt Brecht's *Mother Courage and Her Children* and has written three novels, *Sassafrass, Cypress and Indigo, Betsey Brown* and *Liliane*. Her poetry includes *nappy edges, A Daughter's Geography, Ridin' the Moon in Texas* and *From Okra to Greens*.

NTOZAKE SHANGE

Plays: 1

for colored girls who have considered suicide/
when the rainbow is enuf
spell #7
The Love Space Demands

with introductions by the author

Methuen Drama

METHUEN CONTEMPORARY DRAMATISTS

This collection first published in Great Britain in 1992
by Methuen Drama

Methuen Publishing Ltd
215 Vauxhall Bridge Road
London SW1V 1EJ

www.methuen.co.uk

Methuen Publishing Ltd reg. number 3543167

for colored girls who have considered suicide / when the rainbow is enough
first published in Great Britain in 1978 by Eyre Methuen Ltd, reprinted 1984 and
1988 by Methuen London Ltd and reprinted in 1990 by Methuen Drama
Copyright © 1977 by Ntozake Shange

spell #7 first published in Great Britain in 1982 by Penguin Books in
Three Pieces, first published in this edition in 1985 by Methuen London Ltd,
reprinted in 1990 by Methuen Drama
Copyright © 1981, 1982, 1985 by Ntozake Shange

The Love Space Demands: A Continuing Saga
first published in Great Britain in this edition in 1992
Copyright © 1987, 1991, 1992 by Ntozake Shange

This collection copyright © 1992 by Ntozake Shange

The author has asserted her moral rights

A CIP catalogue record for this book is available at the British Library.

ISBN 0 413 67370 7

Transferred to digital printing 2002.

Contents

Ntozake Shange: A Chronology

Plays

1974 *for colored girls who have considered suicide when the rainbow is enuf* first performed in the USA at the Bacchanal in Berkeley, Calif., 1974 and on Broadway, 1976. First version published in the USA by Shameless Hussy Press, 1975 and second version by Macmillan Publishing, 1977; published in the UK by Eyre Methuen 1978.

1977 *A Photograph: Lovers in Motion* first performed in the USA in 1977.

1979 *spell #7* first performed in the USA by Joseph Papp's Public Theatre, New York in 1979; first British performance by the Women's Playhouse Trust at the Donmar Warehouse, London, 1985. Published in the UK by Penguin in *Three Pieces*, 1985 and by Methuen London in 1990.

1980 *Boogie Woogie Landscapes* first performed in the USA in 1980.

1991 *The Love Space Demands* first performed in the USA in 1991; first UK performance at Cochrane Theatre, London, 1992. Published in the USA by St Martin's Press, 1991; published in the UK by Methuen Drama, 1992.

Poetry

1974 *From Okra to Greens*, first performed in the USA in 1985. Published in the USA by Coffee House Press, 1974.

1979 *nappy edges* published in the USA by St Martin's Press, 1979 and in the UK by Methuen London, 1986.

1982 *A Daughter's Geography*, first performed in USA in 1982. Published in the USA by St Martin's Press, 1984; published in the UK by Methuen London, 1984.

1987 *Ridin' the Moon in Texas* first performed in the USA in 1985. Published in the USA by St Martin's Press, 1987.

Fiction and Non-fiction

for colored girls who have considered suicide/ when the rainbow is enuf

for the spirits of my grandma
viola benzena murray owens
and my great aunt
effie owens josey

*for colored girls who have considered suicide/ when the rainbow
is enuf* was first presented at the Bacchanal, a woman's bar
just outside Berkeley, California. With Paula Moss & Elvia Marta
who worked with me in Raymond Sawyer's Afro-American
Dance Company & Halifu's The Spirit of Dance; Nashira Ntosha,
a guitarist & program coordinator at KPOO-FM (one of the
few Bay Area stations focusing on women's programming);
Jessica Hagedorn, a poet & reading tour companion; & Joanna
Griffin, co-founder of the Bacchanal, publisher of Effie's Press, &
a poet. We just did it. Working in bars waz a circumstantial
aesthetic of poetry in San Francisco from Spec's, an old beat
hangout, to 'new' Malvina's, Minnie's Can-Do Club, the Coffee
Gallery, & the Rippletad. With as much space as a small studio on
the Lower East Side, the five of us, five women, proceeded
to dance, make poems, make music, make a woman's theater for
about twenty patrons. This was December of 1974. We were
a little raw, self-conscious, & eager. Whatever we were discover-
ing in ourselves that nite had been in process among us for
almost two years.

I first met Jessica & Nashira thru Third World Communications
(The Woman's Collective) when the first anthology of Third
World women writers in the U.S.A. was published. With Janice
Mirikitani, Avotcja, Carol Lee Sanchez, Janet Campbell Hale,
Kitty Tsui, Janic Cobb, Thulani, and a score more, San Francisco
waz inundated with women poets, women's readings, & a multi-
lingual woman presence, new to all of us & desperately
appreciated. The force of these readings on all our lives waz to

become evident as we directed our energies toward clarifying our
lives—& the lives of our mothers, daughters, & grandmothers—
as women. During the same period, Shameless Hussy Press & The
Oakland Women's Press Collective were also reading anywhere
& everywhere they could. In a single season, Susan Griffin,
Judy Grahn, Barbara Gravelle, & Alta, were promoting the poetry
& presence of women in a legendary male-poet's environment.
This is the energy & part of the style that nurtured *for colored
girls* . . .

More stable as a source of inspiration & historical continuity waz
the Women's Studies Program at Sonoma State College, where
I worked with J. J. Wilson, Joanna Griffin, & Wopo Holup over a
three year span. Courses designed to make women's lives &
dynamics familiar to us, such as: Woman as Artist; Woman as
Poet; Androgynous Myths in Literature; Women's Biography I & II;
Third World Women Writers, are inextricably bound to the
development of my sense of the world, myself, & women's language. Studying the mythology of women from antiquity to the
present day led directly to the piece *Sechita* in which a dance
hall girl is perceived as deity, as slut, as innocent & knowing.
Unearthing the mislaid, forgotten, &/or misunderstood women
writers, painters, mothers, cowgirls, & union leaders of our
pasts proved to be both a supportive experience & a challenge not
to let them down, not to do less than—at all costs not be less
woman than—our mothers, from Isis to Marie Laurencin, Zora
Neale Hurtson to Kathe Kollwitz, Anna May Wong to
Calamity Jane.

Such joy & excitement I knew in Sonoma, then I would commute
back the sixty miles to San Francisco to study dance with
Raymond Sawyer, Ed Mock, & Halifu. Knowing a woman's mind
& spirit had been allowed me, with dance I discovered my body
more intimately than I had imagined possible. With the
acceptance of the ethnicity of my thighs & backside, came a clearer
understanding of my voice as a woman & as a poet. The freedom
to move in space, to demand of my own sweat a perfection
that could continually be approached, though never known, waz
poem to me, my body & mind ellipsing, probably for the first
time in my life. Just as Women's Studies had rooted me to an
articulated female heritage & imperative, so dance as explicated
by Raymond Sawyer & Ed Mock insisted that everything African,
everything halfway colloquial, a grimace, a strut, an arched
back over a yawn, waz mine. I moved what waz my unconscious
knowledge of being in a colored woman's body to my known
everydayness. The depth of my past waz made tangible to me in
Sawyer's *Ananse*, a dance exploring the Diaspora to contemporary
Senegalese music, pulling ancient trampled spirits out of present
tense Afro-American Dance. Watching Ed Mock re-create the
Step Brothers' or Bert Williams' routines in class or on stage, in
black face mimicking Eddie Cantor or Gloria Swanson, being
the rush of irony & control that are the foundation of jazz dance,
was as startling as humbling. With Raymond Sawyer & Ed Mock,
Paula Moss & I learned the wealth of our bodies, if we worked,
if we opened up, if we made the dance our own.

The first experience of women's theater for me as a performer

waz the months I spent with Halifu Osumare's The Spirit of
Dance, a troupe of five to six black women who depicted the
history of Black dance from its origins in Western Africa thru to
the popular dances seen on our streets. Without a premeditated or
conscious desire to create a female piece, that's what, in fact,
Halifu did. Working in San Francisco & Berkeley public schools
as an adjunct to Ethnic Studies, I learned the mechanics of self-
production & absorbed some of Halifu's confidence in her work,
the legitimacy of our visions. After some 73 performances
with The Spirit of Dance, I left the company to begin production
of *for colored girls* . . .

In the summer of 1974 I had begun a series of seven poems,
modeled on Judy Grahn's *The Common Woman*, which were to
explore the realities of seven different kinds of women. They
were numbered pieces: the women were to be nameless & assume
hegemony as dictated by the fullness of their lives. The first of
the series is the poem, 'one' (orange butterflies & aqua sequins),
which prompted the title *& this is for colored girls who have
considered suicide/ when the rainbow is enuf.* I waz smitten by
my own language, & called all the performances I waz to give
from then on by that title. In other words, all the readings &
choreopoetry that Paula Moss & I developed after that summer waz
for colored girls. . . . We started at the Bacchanal & worked
through the winter at Ed Mock's Dance Studio with the assistance
of West Coast Dance Works, setting pieces & cleaning up
poems. I found two bands, The Sound Clinic (a horn trio) &
Jean Desarmes & His Raggae Blues Band, who agreed to work with

us if I found space. & I did. The space we used waz the space
I knew: Women's Studies Departments, bars, cafes, & poetry
centers. With the selection of poems changing, dependent upon our
audience & our mood, & the dance growing to take space of its
own, so that Paula inspired my words to fall from me with her
body, & The Sound Clinic working with new arrangements of
Ornette Coleman compositions & their own, The Raggae Blues
Band giving Caribbean renditions of Jimi Hendrix & Redding, we
set dates for Minnie's Can-Do Club in Haight-Ashbury. The
poets showed up for us, the dancers showed up for us, the
women's community showed up, & we were listed as a 'must see'
in *The Bay Guardian*. Eight days after our last weekend
at Minnie's, Paula & I left to drive cross country to New York
to do 'the show,' as we called it, at the Studio Rivbea
in New York.

Our work in San Francisco waz over. With the courage of
children, we staged the same sort of informal & improvised cho-
reopoems at Rivbea during the Summer Music Festival. Instead
of the Standing-Room-Only crowds we were accustomed to in San
Francisco, my family & a few friends came to see our great
project. One of these friends, Oz Scott, & my sister, Ifa Iyaun,
who were instrumental in the development of *for colored girls* . . .
saw the show that night. Oz offered to help me with the staging
of the work for a New York audience, since Paula & I obviously
didn't understand some things. We moved from the Rivbea
to the Old Reliable on East 3rd Street to work through some of the
ideas Oz had & the new things Paula & I were developing.

Gylan Kain of the Original Last Poets waz working there every
Monday night. We worked with him & any other poets &
dancers who showed up. Several members of the original New
York show came to us just this haphazardly. Aku Kadogo & I both
had scholarships at Diane McIntyre's Sounds-in-Motion Dance
Studio. I asked her if she felt like improvising on the Lower
East Side, she agreed & has been with the show ever since.
Laurie Carlos stopped by one evening. She stayed. Somehow
word got out & people started coming to the back room of this
neighborhood bar. We were moved to a new bar down the street,
DeMonte's, after eleven weeks of no-pay hard-work three sets
a night—maybe a shot of cognac on the house.

The show at DeMonte's waz prophetic. By this time, December
of 1975, we had weaned the piece of extraneous theatricality,
enlisted Trazana Beverley, Laurie Carlos, Laurie Hayes, Aku
Kadogo, & of course, Paula & I were right there. The most prescient
change in the concept of the work waz that I gave up directorial
powers to Oz Scott. By doing this, I acknowledged that the
poems & the dance worked on their own to do & be what they
were. As opposed to viewing the pieces as poems, I came to
understand these twenty-odd poems as a single statement, a
choreopoem.

We finally hit at DeMonte's. Those institutions I had shunned as
a poet—producers, theaters, actresses, & sets—now were
essential to us. *for colored girls who have considered suicide/
when the rainbow is enuf* waz a theater piece. Woody King

picked up our option to produce us as a Workshop under Equity's
Showcase Code at Henry Street. With the assistance of the
New York Shakespeare Festival & Joe Papp, we received space &
a set, lights & a mailing list, things Paula & I had done without
for two years. We opened at Henry Street with two new actress-
dancers, Thea Martinez & Judy Dearing. Lines of folks & talk
all over the Black & Latin community propelled us to the Public
Theater in June. Then to the Booth Theater on Broadway in
September of 1976.

Every move we've made since the first showing of *for colored
girls* . . . in California has demanded changes of text, personnel, &
staging. The final production at the Booth is as close to distilled
as any of us in all our art forms can make it. With two new
actresses, Janet League & Rise Collins, & with the help of Seret
Scott, Michelle Shay, & Roxanne Reese, the rest of the cast is
enveloping almost 6,000 people a week in the words of a young
black girl's growing up, her triumphs & errors, our struggle to
become all that is forbidden by our environment, all that is
forfeited by our gender, all that we have forgotten.

I had never imagined not doing *for colored girls*. . . . It waz just
my poems, any poems I happened to have. Now I have left the
show on Broadway, to write poems, stories, plays, my dreams.
for colored girls . . . is either too big for my off-off Broadway
taste, or too little for my exaggerated sense of freedom, held over
from seven years of improvised poetry readings. Or, perhaps,
the series has actually finished itself. Poems come on their own

time: i am offering these to you as what i've received from this world so far.

i am on the other side of the rainbow/ picking up the pieces of days spent waitin for the poem to be heard/ while you listen/ i have other work to do/

ntozake shange
new york, 1976

for colored girls who
have considered suicide/
when the rainbow is enuf

lady in brown
dark phrases of womanhood
of never havin been a girl
half-notes scattered
without rhythm/ no tune
distraught laughter fallin
over a black girl's shoulder
it's funny/ it's hysterical
the melody-less-ness of her dance
don't tell nobody don't tell a soul
she's dancin on beer cans & shingles

this must be the spook house
another song with no singers
lyrics/ no voices

& interrupted solos
unseen performances

are we ghouls?
children of horror?
the joke?

don't tell nobody don't tell a soul
are we animals? have we gone crazy?

i can't hear anythin
but maddening screams
& the soft strains of death
& you promised me
you promised me . . .
somebody/ anybody
sing a black girl's song
bring her out
to know herself
to know you
but sing her rhythms
carin/ struggle/ hard times
sing her song of life
she's been dead so long
closed in silence so long
she doesn't know the sound
of her own voice
her infinite beauty

4

she's half-notes scattered
without rhythm/no tune
sing her sighs
sing the song of her possibilities
sing a righteous gospel
the makin of a melody
let her be born
let her be born
            & handled warmly.

    lady in brown
i'm outside chicago

    lady in yellow
i'm outside detroit

    lady in purple
i'm outside houston

    lady in red
i'm outside baltimore

    lady in green
i'm outside san francisco

    lady in blue
i'm outside manhattan

    lady in orange
i'm outside st. louis

lady in brown
& this is for colored girls who have considered suicide
but moved to the ends of their own rainbows.

everyone
mama's little baby likes shortnin, shortnin,
mama's little baby likes shortnin bread
mama's little baby likes shortnin, shortnin,
mama's little baby likes shortnin bread

little sally walker, sittin in a saucer
rise, sally, rise, wipe your weepin eyes
an put your hands on your hips
an let your backbone slip
o, shake it to the east
o, shake it to the west
shake it to the one
that you like the best

lady in purple
you're it

*As the lady in brown tags each of
the other ladies they freeze. When
each one has been tagged the lady
in brown freezes. Immediately
"Dancing in the Streets" by Martha
and the Vandellas is heard. All*

of the ladies start to dance. The
lady in green, the lady in blue, and
the lady in yellow do the pony,
the big boss line, the swim, and
the nose dive. The other ladies
dance in place.

lady in yellow
it was graduation nite & i waz the only virgin in the crowd
bobby mills martin jerome & sammy yates eddie jones & randi
all cousins
all the prettiest niggers in this factory town
carried me out wit em
in a deep black buick
smellin of thunderbird & ladies in heat
we rambled from camden to mount holly
laughin at the afternoon's speeches
& danglin our tassles from the rear view mirror
climbin different sorta project stairs
movin toward snappin beer cans &
GET IT GET IT THAT'S THE WAY TO DO IT MAMA
all mercer county graduated the same nite
         cosmetology secretarial pre-college autoshop & business
all us movin from mama to what ever waz out there

that nite we raced a big ol truck from the barbeque stand
trying to tell him bout the party at jacqui's
where folks graduated last year waz waitin to hit it wid us

7

i got drunk & cdnt figure out
whose hand waz on my thigh/ but it didn't matter
cuz these cousins martin eddie sammy jerome & bobby
waz my sweethearts alternately since the seventh grade
& everybody knew i always started cryin if somebody actually
tried to take advantage of me
        at jacqui's
ulinda mason was stickin her mouth all out
while we tumbled out the buick
eddie jones waz her lickin stick
but i knew how to dance
        it got soo hot
vincent ramos puked all in the punch
& harly jumped all in tico's face
cuz he was leavin for the navy in the mornin
hadda kick ass so we'd all remember how bad he waz
seems like sheila & marguerite waz fraid
to get their hair turnin back
so they laid up against the wall
lookin almost sexy
didnt wanna sweat
but me & my fellas   we waz dancin

since 1963 i'd won all kinda contests
wid the cousins at the POLICE ATHLETIC LEAGUE DANCES
all mercer county knew
any kin to martin yates cd turn somersaults
fore smokey robinson cd get a woman excited

we danced   doin nasty ol tricks

> *The lady in yellow sings along*
> *with the Dells for a moment. The*
> *lady in orange and the lady in blue*
> *jump up and parody the lady in*
> *yellow and the Dells. The lady in*
> *yellow stares at them. They sit down.*

doin nasty ol tricks i'd been thinkin since may
cuz graduation nite had to be hot
& i waz the only virgin
so i hadda make like my hips waz inta some business
that way everybody thot whoever was gettin it
was a older man cdnt run the streets wit youngsters
martin slipped his leg round my thigh
the dells bumped "stay"
up & down—up & down the new carver homes
WE WAZ GROWN   WE WAZ FINALLY GROWN

ulinda alla sudden went crazy
went over to eddie cursin & carryin on
tearin his skin wid her nails
the cousins tried to talk sense to her
tried to hold her arms
lissin bitch sammy went on

9

bobby whispered i shd go wit him
fore they go ta cuttin
fore the police arrived
we teetered silently thru the parkin lot
no un uhuh
we didn't know nothin bout no party
bobby started lookin at me
yeah
he started looking at me real strange
like i waz a woman or somethin/
started talkin real soft
in the backseat of that ol buick
WOW
by daybreak
i just cdnt stop grinnin.

*The Dells singing "Stay" comes in
and all of the ladies except the lady
in blue join in and sing along.*

lady in blue
you gave it up in a buick?

lady in yellow
yeh, and honey, it was wonderful.

lady in green
we used to do it all up in the dark
in the corners . . .

10

lady in blue
some niggah sweating all over you.

lady in red
it was good!

lady in blue
i never did like to grind.

lady in yellow
what other kind of dances are there?

lady in blue
mambo, bomba, merengue

when i waz sixteen i ran off to the south bronx
cuz i waz gonna meet up wit willie colon
& dance all the time
                    mamba bomba merengue
lady in yellow
do you speak spanish?

lady in blue
olà
my papa thot he was puerto rican & we wda been
cept we waz just reglar niggahs wit hints of spanish
so off i made it to this 36 hour marathon dance
con salsa con ricardo
'suggggggggggar' ray on southern blvd

next door to this fotografi place
jammed wit burial weddin & communion relics
next door to la real ideal genuine spanish barber
                    up up up up up stairs & stairs & lotsa hallway
wit my colored new jersey self
didn't know what anybody waz saying
cept if dancin waz proof of origin
            i was jibarita herself that nite
& the next day
i kept smilin & right on steppin
if he cd lead i waz ready to dance
if he cdnt lead
i caught this attitude
            i'd seen rosa do
& wd not be bothered
i waz twirlin hippin givin much quik feet
& bein a mute cute colored puerto rican
til saturday afternoon when the disc-jockey say
'SORRY FOLKS WILLIE COLON AINT GONNA MAKE IT TODAY'
& alla my niggah temper came outta control
& i wdnt dance wit nobody
& i talked english loud
& i love you more than i waz mad
uh huh uh huh
more than more than
when i discovered archie shepp & subtle blues
doncha know i wore out the magic of juju
heroically resistin being possessed

oooooooooooooh the sounds
sneakin in under age to slug's
to stare ata real 'artiste'
& every word outta imamu's mouth waz gospel
& if jesus cdnt play a horn like shepp
waznt no need for colored folks to bear no cross at all

& poem is my thank-you for music
& i love you more than poem
more than aureliano buendia loved macondo
more than hector lavoe loved himself
more than the lady loved gardenias
more than celia loves cuba or graciela loves el son
more than the flamingoes shoo-do-n-doo-wah love bein pretty

oyè négro
te amo mas que   te amo mas que
when you play
yr flute

    everyone (very softly)
te amo mas que   te amo mas que

    lady in red
without any assistance or guidance from you
i have loved you assiduously for 8 months 2 wks & a day
i have been stood up four times
i've left 7 packages on yr doorstep

forty poems 2 plants & 3 handmade notecards i left
town so i cd send to you have been no help to me
on my job
you call at 3:00 in the mornin on weekdays
so i cd drive 27½ miles cross the bay before i go to work
charmin charmin
but you are of no assistance
i want you to know
this waz an experiment
to see how selfish i cd be
if i wd really carry on to snare a possible lover
if i waz capable of debasin my self for the love of another
if i cd stand not being wanted
when i wanted to be wanted
& i cannot
so
with no further assistance & no guidance from you
i am endin this affair

this note is attached to a plant
i've been waterin since the day i met you
you may water it
yr damn self

    lady in orange
i dont wanna write
in english or spanish
i wanna sing   make you dance
like the bata   dance   scream

twitch hips wit me cuz
i done forgot all abt words
aint got no definitions
i wanna whirl
                    with you

                         Music starts, "Che Che Cole" by
                         Willie Colon.
                         Everyone starts to dance.

our whole body
wrapped like a ripe mango
ramblin whippin thru space
on the corner in the park
where the rug useta be
let willie colon take you out
swing your head
push your leg to the moon with me

i'm on the lower east side
in new york city
and i can't   i can't
talk witchu no more

    lady in yellow
we gotta dance to keep from cryin

    lady in brown
we gotta dance to keep from dyin

15

lady in red
so come on

lady in brown
come on

lady in purple
come on

lady in orange
hold yr head like it was ruby sapphire
i'm a poet
who writes in english
come to share the worlds witchu

everyone
come to share our worlds witchu
we come here to be dancin
            to be dancin
        to be dancin
        baya

> *There is a sudden light change, all
> of the ladies react as if they had
> been struck in the face. The lady in
> green and the lady in yellow run
> out up left, the lady in orange runs
> out the left volm, the lady in
> brown runs out up right.*

16

lady in blue
a friend is hard to press charges against

lady in red
if you know him
you must have wanted it

lady in purple
a misunderstanding

lady in red
you know
these things happen

lady in blue
are you sure
you didnt suggest

lady in purple
had you been drinkin

lady in red
a rapist is always to be a stranger
to be legitimate
someone you never saw
a man wit obvious problems

lady in purple
pin-ups attached to the insides of his lapels

lady in blue
ticket stubs from porno flicks in his pocket

lady in purple
a lil dick

lady in red
or a strong mother

lady in blue
or just a brutal virgin

lady in red
but if you've been seen in public wit him
danced one dance
kissed him good-bye lightly

lady in purple
wit closed mouth

lady in blue
pressin charges will be as hard
as keepin yr legs closed
while five fools try to run a train on you

lady in red
these men friends of ours
who smile nice

18

stay employed
and take us out to dinner

    lady in purple
lock the door behind you

    lady in blue
wit fist in face
to fuck

    lady in red
who make elaborate mediterranean dinners
& let the art ensemble carry all ethical burdens
while they invite a coupla friends over to have you
are sufferin from latent rapist bravado
& we are left wit the scars

    lady in blue
bein betrayed by men who know us

    lady in purple
& expect
like the stranger
we always thot waz comin

    lady in blue
that we will submit

lady in purple
we must have known

lady in red
women relinquish all personal rights
in the presence of a man
who apparently cd·be considered a rapist

lady in purple
especially if he has been considered a friend

lady in blue
& is no less worthy of bein beat witin an inch of his life
bein publicly ridiculed
havin two fists shoved up his ass

lady in red
than the stranger
we always thot it wd be

lady in blue
who never showed up

lady in red
cuz it turns out the nature of rape has changed

lady in blue
we can now meet them in circles we frequent for companionship

lady in purple
we see them at the coffeehouse

lady in blue
wit someone else we know

lady in red
we cd even have em over for dinner
& get raped in our own houses
by invitation
a friend

> *The lights change, and the ladies*
> *are all hit by an imaginary slap, the*
> *lady in red runs off up left.*

lady in blue
eyes

lady in purple
mice

lady in blue
womb

lady in blue & lady in purple
nobody

> *The lady in purple exits up right.*

21

lady in blue
tubes tables white washed windows
grime from age wiped over once
legs spread
anxious
eyes crawling up on me
eyes rollin in my thighs
metal horses gnawin my womb
dead mice fall from my mouth
i really didnt mean to
i really didnt think i cd
just one day off . . .
get offa me alla this blood
bones shattered like soft ice-cream cones

i cdnt have people
lookin at me
pregnant
i cdnt have my friends see this
dyin danglin tween my legs
& i didnt say a thing
not a sigh
or a fast scream
to get
those eyes offa me
get them steel rods outta me
this hurts
this hurts me

& nobody came
cuz nobody knew
once i waz pregnant & shamed of myself.

> *The lady in blue exits stage left*
> *volm.*

> *Soft deep music is heard, voices*
> *calling "Sechita" come from the*
> *wings and volms. The lady in*
> *purple enters from up right.*

lady in purple
once there were quadroon balls/ elegance in st. louis/ laced
mulattoes/ gamblin down the mississippi/ to memphis/ new
orleans n okra crepes near the bayou/ where the poor white trash
wd sing/ moanin/ strange/ liquid tones/ thru the swamps/

> *The lady in green enters from the*
> *right volm; she is Sechita and for*
> *the rest of the poem dances out*
> *Sechita's life.*

sechita had heard these things/ she moved
as if she'd known them/ the silver n high-toned laughin/
the violins n marble floors/ sechita pushed the clingin
delta dust wit painted toes/ the patch-work tent waz
poka-dotted/ stale lights snatched at the shadows/ creole

23

carnival waz playin natchez in ten minutes/ her splendid
red garters/ gin-stained n itchy on her thigh/ blk-diamond
stockings darned wit yellow threads/ an ol starched taffeta
can-can fell abundantly orange/ from her waist round the
splinterin chair/ sechita/ egyptian/ goddess of creativity/
2nd millennium/ threw her heavy hair in a coil over her neck/
sechita/ goddess/ the recordin of history/ spread crimson oil
on her cheeks/ waxed her eyebrows/ n unconsciously slugged
the last hard whiskey in the glass/ the broken mirror she
used to decorate her face/ made her forehead tilt backwards/
her cheeks appear sunken/ her sassy chin only large enuf/
to keep her full lower lip/ from growin into her neck/ sechita/
had learned to make allowances for the distortions/
but the heavy dust of the delta/ left a tinge of grit n
darknëss/ on every one of her dresses/ on her arms & her
shoulders/ sechita/ waz anxious to get back to st. louis/
the dirt there didnt crawl from the earth into yr soul/
at least/ in st. louis/ the grime waz store bought
second-hand/ here in natchez/ god seemed to be wipin his
feet in her face/

one of the wrestlers had finally won
tonite/ the mulatto/ raul/ was sposed to hold the boomin
half-caste/ searin eagle/ in a bear hug/ 8 counts/ get
thrown unawares/ fall out the ring/ n then do searin eagle
in for good/ sechita/ cd hear redneck whoops n slappin on
the back/ she gathered her sparsely sequined skirts/ tugged
the waist cincher from under her greyin slips/ n made her face

immobile/ she made her face like nefertiti/ approachin her
own tomb/ she suddenly threw/ her leg full-force/ thru the
canvas curtain/ a deceptive glass stone/ sparkled/ malignant
on her ankle/ her calf waz tauntin in the brazen carnie
lights/ the full moon/ sechita/ goddess/ of love/ egypt/
2nd millennium/ performin the rites/ the conjurin of men/
conjurin the spirit/ in natchez/ the mississippi spewed
a heavy fume of barely movin waters/ sechita's legs slashed
furiously thru the cracker nite/ & gold pieces hittin the
makeshift stage/ her thighs/ they were aimin coins tween her
thighs/ sechita/ egypt/ goddess/ harmony/ kicked viciously
thru the nite/ catchin stars tween her toes.

*The lady in green exits into the
stage left volm, the lady in purple
exits into up stage left.*

*The lady in brown enters from up
stage right.*

lady in brown
de library waz right down from de trolly tracks
cross from de laundry-mat
thru de big shinin floors & granite pillars
ol st. louis is famous for
i found toussaint
but not til after months uv
cajun katie/ pippi longstockin

christopher robin/ eddie heyward & a pooh bear
in the children's room
only pioneer girls & magic rabbits
& big city white boys
i knew i waznt sposedta
but i ran inta the ADULT READING ROOM
              & came across

               TOUSSAINT

               my first blk man
(i never counted george washington carver
cuz i didnt like peanuts)
               ·   still
TOUSSAINT waz a blk man a negro like my mama say
who refused to be a slave
& he spoke french
& didnt low no white man to tell him nothin
             not napolean
             not maximillien
             not robespierre

TOUSSAINT L'OUVERTURE
waz the beginnin uv reality for me
in the summer contest for
who colored child can read
15 books in three weeks
i won & raved abt TOUSSAINT L'OUVERTURE
at the afternoon ceremony

waz disqualified
            cuz Toussaint
                  belonged in the ADULT READING ROOM
                        & i cried
& carried dead Toussaint home in the book
he waz dead & livin to me
cuz TOUSSAINT & them
they held the citadel gainst the french
wid the spirits of ol dead africans from outta the ground
TOUSSAINT led they army of zombies
walkin cannon ball shootin spirits to free Haiti
& they waznt slaves no more

                  TOUSSAINT L'OUVERTURE
became my secret lover at the age of 8
i entertained him in my bedroom
widda flashlight under my covers
way inta the night/ we discussed strategies
how to remove white girls from my hopscotch games
& etc.
TOUSSAINT
waz layin in bed wit me next to raggedy ann
the night i decided to run away from my
                  integrated home
                  integrated street
                  integrated school
1955 waz not a good year for lil blk girls

Toussaint said 'lets go to haiti'

i said 'awright'
& packed some very important things in a brown paper bag
so i wdnt haveta come back
then Toussaint & i took the hodiamont streetcar
to the river
last stop
only 15¢
cuz there waznt nobody cd see Toussaint cept me
& we walked all down thru north st. louis
where the french settlers usedta live
in tiny brick houses all huddled together
wit barely missin windows & shingles uneven
wit colored kids playin & women on low porches sippin beer

i cd talk to Toussaint down by the river
like this waz where we waz gonna stow away
on a boat for new orleans
& catch a creole fishin-rig for port-au-prince
then we waz just gonna read & talk all the time
& eat fried bananas
                    we waz just walkin & skippin past ol drunk men
when dis ol young boy jumped out at me sayin
'HEY GIRL YA BETTAH COME OVAH HEAH N TALK TO ME'
well
i turned to TOUSSAINT (who waz furious)
& i shouted
'ya silly ol boy
ya bettah leave me alone

or TOUSSAINT'S gonna get yr ass'
de silly ol boy came round de corner laughin all in my face
'yellah gal
ya sure must be somebody to know my name so quick'
i waz disgusted
& wanted to get on to haiti
widout some tacky ol boy botherin me
still he kept standin there
kickin milk cartons & bits of brick
tryin to get all in my business
                         i mumbled to L'OUVERTURE 'what shd I do'
finally
i asked this silly ol boy
'WELL WHO ARE YOU?'
he say
'MY NAME IS TOUSSAINT JONES'
well
i looked right at him
those skidded out cordoroy pants
a striped teashirt wid holes in both elbows
a new scab over his left eye
& i said
                     'what's yr name again'
he say
'i'm toussaint jones'
'wow
i am on my way to see
TOUSSAINT L'OUVERTURE in HAITI

are ya any kin to him
he dont take no stuff from no white folks
& they gotta country all they own
& there aint no slaves'
that silly ol boy squinted his face all up
'looka heah girl
i am TOUSSAINT JONES
& i'm right heah lookin at ya
& i dont take no stuff from no white folks
ya dont see none round heah do ya?'
& he sorta pushed out his chest
then he say
'come on   lets go on down to the docks
& look at the boats'
i waz real puzzled goin down to the docks
wit my paper bag & my books
i felt TOUSSAINT L'OUVERTURE sorta leave me
& i waz sad
til i realized
TOUSSAINT JONES waznt too different
from TOUSSAINT L'OUVERTURE
cept the ol one waz in haiti
& this one wid me speakin english & eatin apples
yeah.
toussaint jones waz awright wit me
no tellin what all spirits we cd move
down by the river
st. louis 1955   hey wait.

The lady in brown exits into the
stage right volm.

The lady in red enters from the
stage left volm.

    lady in red
orange butterflies & aqua sequins
ensconsed tween slight bosoms
silk roses dartin from behind her ears
the passion flower of southwest los angeles
meandered down hoover street
past dark shuttered houses where
women from louisiana shelled peas
round 3:00 & sent their sons
whistlin to the store for fatback & black-eyed peas
she glittered in heat
& seemed to be lookin for rides
when she waznt & absolutely
eyed every man who waznt lame white or noddin out
she let her thigh slip from her skirt
crossin the street
she slowed to be examined
& she never looked back to smile
or acknowledge a sincere 'hey mama'
or to meet the eyes of someone
purposely findin sometin to do in

her direction
                she waz sullen
                & the rhinestones etchin the corners of her mouth
                suggested tears
                fresh kisses that had done no good
she always wore her stomach out
lined with small iridescent feathers
the hairs round her navel seemed to dance
& she didnt let on
she knew
from behind her waist waz aching to be held
the pastel ivy drawn on her shoulders
to be brushed with lips & fingers
smellin of honey & jack daniels
                she waz hot
                a deliberate coquette
                who never did without
                what she wanted
& she wanted to be unforgettable
she wanted to be a memory
a wound   to every man
arragant enough to want her
                she waz the wrath
                of women in windows
                    fingerin shades/ ol lace curtains
                    camoflagin despair &
                    stretch marks
so she glittered honestly

delighted she waz desired
& allowed those especially
schemin/ tactful suitors
to experience her body & spirit
tearin/ so easily blendin with theirs/
& they were so happy
& lay on her lime sheets full & wet
from her tongue   she kissed
them reverently   even ankles
edges of beards . . .

The stage goes to darkness except
for a special on the lady in red,
who lies motionless on the floor; as
the lights slowly fade up the lady
in red sits up.

at 4:30 AM
she rose
movin the arms & legs that trapped her
she sighed affirmin the sculptured man
& made herself a bath
of dark musk oil egyptian crystals
& florida water to remove his smell
to wash away the glitter
to watch the butterflies melt into
suds & the rhinestones fall beneath
her buttocks like smooth pebbles

33

in a missouri creek
layin in water
she became herself
ordinary
brown braided woman
with big legs & full lips
reglar
seriously intendin to finish her
night's work
she quickly walked to her guest
straddled on her pillows & began

       'you'll have to go now/ i've
       a lot of work to do/ & i cant
       with a man around/ here are yr pants/
       there's coffee on the stove/ its been
       very nice/ but i cant see you again/
       you got what you came for/ didnt you'

& she smiled
he wd either mumble curses bout crazy bitches
or sit dumbfounded
while she repeated

       'i cdnt possibly wake up/ with
       a strange man in my bed/ why
       dont you go home'

she cda been slapped upside the head
or verbally challenged
but she never waz
& the ones who fell prey to the

dazzle of hips painted with
orange blossoms & magnolia scented wrists
had wanted no more
than to lay between her sparklin thighs
& had planned on leavin before dawn
& she had been so divine
devastatingly bizarre the way
her mouth fit round
& now she stood a
reglar colored girl
fulla the same malice
livid indifference as a sistah
worn from supportin a wd be hornplayer
or waitin by the window

                              & they knew
                              & left in a hurry

she wd gather her tinsel &
jewels from the tub
& laugh gayly or vengeful
she stored her silk roses by her bed
& when she finished writin
the account of her exploit in a diary
embroidered with lilies & moonstones
she placed the rose behind her ear
& cried herself to sleep.

All the lights fade except for a special on the lady in red; the lady in red exits into the stage left volm.

The lady in blue enters from up right.

   lady in blue
i usedta live in the world
then i moved to HARLEM
& my universe is now six blocks

when i walked in the pacific
i imagined waters ancient from accra/ tunis
cleansin me/ feedin me
now my ankles are coated in grey filth
from the puddle neath the hydrant

my oceans were life
what waters i have here sit stagnant
circlin ol men's bodies
shit & broken lil whiskey bottles
left to make me bleed

i usedta live in the world
now i live in harlem & my universe is six blocks
a tunnel with a train
i can ride anywhere
remaining a stranger

NO MAN YA CANT GO WIT ME/ I DONT EVEN
KNOW YOU/ NO/ I DONT WANNA KISS YOU/
YOU AINT BUT 12 YRS OLD/ NO MAN/ PLEASE
PLEASE PLEASE LEAVE ME ALONE/ TOMORROW/ YEAH/
NO/ PLEASE/ I CANT USE IT
  i cd stay alone
  a woman in the world
  then i moved to
HARLEM
i come in at dusk
stay close to the curb

                  The lady in yellow enters, she's
                  waiting for a bus.

round midnite
praying wont no young man
think i'm pretty in a dark mornin

                  The lady in purple enters, she's
                  waiting for a bus.

wdnt be good
not good at all
to meet a tall short black brown young man fulla his power
in the dark
in my universe of six blocks
straight up brick walls
women hangin outta windows

like ol silk stockings
cats cryin/ children gigglin/ a tavern wit red curtains
bad smells/ kissin ladies smilin & dirt
sidewalks spittin/ men cursing/ playin

The lady in orange enters, she is
being followed by a man, the
lady in blue becomes that man.

'I SPENT MORE MONEY YESTERDAY
THAN THE DAY BEFORE & ALL THAT'S MORE N YOU
NIGGAH EVER GOTTA HOLD TO
COME OVER HERE BITCH
CANT YA SEE THIS IS $5'

never mind sister
dont pay him no mind
go go go go go go sister
do yr thing
never mind

i usedta live in the world
really be in the world
free & sweet talkin
good mornin & thank-you & nice day
uh huh
i cant now
i cant be nice to nobody

nice is such a rip-off
reglar beauty & a smile in the street
is just a set-up

i usedta be in the world
a woman in the world
i hadda right to the world
then i moved to harlem
for the set-up
a universe
six blocks of cruelty
piled up on itself
a tunnel
closin

The four ladies on stage freeze,
count 4, then the ladies in
blue, purple, yellow and orange
move to their places for the next
poem.

lady in purple
three of us like a pyramid
three friends
one laugh
one music
one flowered shawl
knotted on each neck

we all saw him at the same time
& he saw us·
i felt a quick thump in each one of us
didnt know what to do
we all wanted what waz comin our way
so we split
but he found one
& she loved him

the other two were tickled
& spurned his advances
when the one who loved him waz somewhere else
he wd come to her saying
yr friends love you very much
i have tried
& they keep askin where are you
she smiled
wonderin how long her friends
wd hold out
he waz what they were lookin for
he bided his time
he waited til romance waned
the three of us made up stories
bout usedta & cda been nice
the season waz dry
no men
no quickies
not one dance or eyes unrelentin

one day after another
cept for the one who loved him
he appeared irregularly
expectin graciousness no matter what
she cut fresh strawberries
her friends callt less frequently
went on hunts for passin fancies
she cdnt figure out what waz happenin
then the rose
she left by his pillow
she found on her friends desk
& there waz nothing to say
she said
i wanna tell you
he's been after me
all the time
says he's free & can explain
what's happenin wit you
is nothin to me
& i dont wanna hurt you
but you know i need someone now
& you know
how wonderful he is

her friend cdnt speak or cry
they hugged & went to where he waz
wit another woman
he said good-bye to one

tol the other he wd call
he smiled a lot

she held her head on her lap
the lap of her sisters soakin up tears
each understandin how much love stood between them
how much love between them
love between them
love like sisters

*Sharp music is heard, each lady
dances as if catching a disease from
the lady next to her, suddenly
they all freeze.*

lady in orange
ever since i realized there waz someone callt
a colored girl an evil woman a bitch or a nag
i been tryin not to be that & leave bitterness
in somebody else's cup/ come to somebody to love me
without deep & nasty smellin scald from lye or bein
left screamin in a street fulla lunatics/ whisperin
slut bitch bitch niggah/ get outta here wit alla that/
i didnt have any of that for you/ i brought you what joy
i found & i found joy/ honest fingers round my face/ with
dead musicians on 78's from cuba/ or live musicians on five
dollar lp's from chicago/ where i have never been/ & i love
willie colon & arsenio rodriquez/ especially cuz i can make

42

the music loud enuf/ so there is no me but dance/ & when
i can dance like that/ there's nothin cd hurt me/ but
i get tired & i haveta come offa the floor & then there's
that woman who hurt you/ who you left/ three or four times/
& just went back/ after you put my heart in the bottom of
yr shoe/ you just walked back to where you hurt/ & i didnt
have nothin/ so i went to where somebody had somethin for me/
but he waznt you/ & i waz on the way back from her house
in the bottom of yr shoe/ so this is not a love poem/ cuz there
are only memorial albums available/ & even charlie mingus
wanted desperately to be a pimp/ & i wont be able to see eddie
palmieri for months/ so this is a requium for myself/ cuz i
have died in a real way/ not wid aqua coffins & du-wop cadillacs/
i used to joke abt when i waz messin round/ but a real dead
lovin is here for you now/ cuz i dont know anymore/ how
to avoid my own face wet wit my tears/ cuz i had convinced
myself colored girls had no right to sorrow/ & i lived
& loved that way & kept sorrow on the curb/ allegedly
for you/ but i know i did it for myself/
i cdnt stand it
i cdnt stand bein sorry & colored at the same time
it's so redundant in the modern world

    lady in purple
i lived wit myths & music waz my ol man & i cd dance
a dance outta time/ a dance wit no partners/ take my
pills & keep right on steppin/ linger in non-english
speakin arms so there waz no possibility of understandin

43

& you YOU
came sayin i am the niggah/ i am the baddest muthafuckah
out there/
i said yes/ this is who i am waitin for
& to come wit you/ i hadta bring everythin
the dance & the terror
the dead musicians & the hope
& those scars i had hidden wit smiles & good fuckin
lay open
& i dont know i dont know any more tricks
i am really colored & really sad sometimes & you hurt me
more than i ever danced outta/ into oblivion isnt far enuf
to get outta this/ i am ready to die like a lily in the
desert/ & i cdnt let you in on it cuz i didnt know/ here
is what i have/ poems/ big thighs/ lil tits/ &
so much love/ will you take it from me this one time/
please this is for you/ arsenio's tres cleared the way
& makes me pure again/ please please/ this is for you
i want you to love me/ let me love you/ i dont wanna
dance wit ghosts/ snuggle lovers i made up in my drunkenness/
lemme love you just like i am/ a colored girl/ i'm finally bein
real/ no longer symmetrical & impervious to pain

   lady in blue
we deal wit emotion too much
so why dont we go on ahead & be white then/
& make everythin dry & abstract wit no rhythm & no
reelin for sheer sensual pleasure/ yes let's go on

44

& be white/ we're right in the middle of it/ no use
holdin out/ holdin onto ourselves/ lets think our
way outta feelin/ lets abstract ourselves some families
& maybe maybe tonite/ i'll find a way to make myself
come witout you/ no fingers or other objects just thot
which isnt spiritual evolution cuz its empty & godliness
is plenty is ripe & fertile/ thinkin wont do me a bit of
good tonite/ i need to be loved/ & havent the audacity
to say
where are you/ & dont know who to say it to

   lady in yellow
i've lost it
touch wit reality/ i dont know who's doin it
i thot i waz but i waz so stupid i waz able to be hurt
& that's not real/ not anymore/ i shd be immune/ if i'm
still alive & that's what i waz discussin/ how i am still
alive & my dependency on other livin beins for love
i survive on intimacy & tomorrow/ that's all i've got goin
& the music waz like smack & you knew abt that
& still refused my dance waz not enuf/ & it waz all i had
but bein alive & bein a woman & bein colored is a metaphysical
dilemma/ i havent conquered yet/ do you see the point
my spirit is too ancient to understand the separation of
soul & gender/ my love is too delicate to have thrown
back on my face

45

*The ladies in red, green, and brown
enter quietly; in the background
all of the ladies except the lady in
yellow are frozen; the lady in
yellow looks at them, walks by
them, touches them; they do not
move.*

lady in yellow
my love is too delicate to have thrown back on my face

*The lady in yellow starts to exit
into the stage right volm. Just as she
gets to the volm, the lady in brown
comes to life.*

lady in brown
my love is too beautiful to have thrown back on my face

lady in purple
my love is too sanctified to have thrown back on my face

lady in blue
my love is too magic to have thrown back on my face

lady in orange
my love is too saturday nite to have thrown back on my face

46

lady in red
my love is too complicated to have thrown back on my face

lady in green
my love is too music to have thrown back on my face

everyone
music
music

> *The lady in green then breaks into*
> *a dance, the other ladies follow*
> *her lead and soon they are all danc-*
> *ing and chanting together.*

lady in green
yank dankka dank dank

everyone
music

lady in green
yank dankka dank dank

everyone
music

lady in green
yank dankka dank dank

47

  everyone (but started by the lady in yellow)
delicate
delicate
delicate

  everyone (but started by the lady in brown)
and beautiful
and beautiful
and beautiful

  everyone (but started by the lady in purple)
oh sanctified
oh sanctified
oh sanctified

  everyone (but started by the lady in blue)
magic
magic
magic

  everyone (but started by the lady in orange)
and saturday nite
and saturday nite
and saturday nite

  everyone (but started by the lady in red)
and complicated
and complicated

and complicated
and complicated
and complicated
and complicated
and complicated
and complicated

The dance reaches a climax and all
of the ladies fall out tired, but full
of life and togetherness.

lady in green
somebody almost walked off wid alla my stuff
not my poems or a dance i gave up in the street
but somebody almost walked off wid alla my stuff
like a kleptomaniac workin hard & forgettin while stealin
this is mine/ this aint yr stuff/
now why dont you put me back & let me hang out in my own self
somebody almost walked off wid alla my stuff
& didnt care enuf to send a note home sayin
i waz late for my solo conversation
or two sizes too small for my own tacky skirts
what can anybody do wit somethin of no value on
a open market/ did you getta dime for my things/
hey man/ where are you goin wid alla my stuff/
this is a woman's trip & i need my stuff/
to ohh & ahh abt/ daddy/ i gotta mainline number
from my own shit/ now wontchu put me back/ & let

49

me play this duet/ wit this silver ring in my nose/
honest to god/ somebody almost run off wit alla my stuff/
& i didnt bring anythin but the kick & sway of it
the perfect ass for my man & none of it is theirs
this is mine/ ntozake 'her own things'/ that's my name/
now give me my stuff/ i see ya hidin my laugh/ & how i
sit wif my legs open sometimes/ to give my crotch
some sunlight/ & there goes my love my toes my chewed
up finger nails/ niggah/ wif the curls in yr hair/
mr. louisiana hot link/ i want my stuff back/
my rhythms & my voice/ open my mouth/ & let me talk ya
outta/ throwin my shit in the sewar/ this is some delicate
leg & whimsical kiss/ i gotta have to give to my choice/
without you runnin off wit alla my shit/
now you cant have me less i give me away/ & i waz
doin all that/ til ya run off on a good thing/
who is this you left me wit/ some simple bitch
widda bad attitude/ i wants my things/
i want my arm wit the hot iron scar/ & my leg wit the
flea bite/ i want my calloused feet & quik language back
in my mouth/ fried plantains/ pineapple pear juice/
sun-ra & joseph & jules/ i want my own things/ how i lived them/
& give me my memories/ how i waz when i waz there/
you cant have them or do nothin wit them/
stealin my shit from me/ dont make it yrs/ makes it stolen/
somebody almost run off wit alla my stuff/ & i waz standin
there/ lookin at myself/ the whole time
& it waznt a spirit took my stuff/ waz a man whose

ego walked round like Rodan's shadow/ waz a man faster
n my innocence/ waz a lover/ i made too much
room for/ almost run off wit alla my stuff/
& i didnt know i'd give it up so quik/ & the one running wit it/
dont know he got it/ & i'm shoutin this is mine/ & he dont
know he got it/ my stuff is the anonymous ripped off treasure
of the year/ did you know somebody almost got away with me/
me in a plastic bag under their arm/ me
danglin on a string of personal carelessness/ i'm spattered wit
mud & city rain/ & no i didnt get a chance to take a douche/
hey man/ this is not your perogative/ i gotta have me in my
pocket/ to get round like a good woman shd/ & make the poem
in the pot or the chicken in the dance/ what i got to do/
i gotta have my stuff to do it to/
why dont ya find yr own things/ & leave this package
of me for my destiny/ what ya got to get from me/
i'll give it to ya/ yeh/ i'll give it to ya/
round 5:00 in the winter/ when the sky is blue-red/
& Dew City is gettin pressed/ if it's really my stuff/
ya gotta give it to me/ if ya really want it/ i'm
the only one/ can handle it

   lady in blue
that niggah will be back tomorrow, sayin 'i'm sorry'

   lady in yellow
get this, last week my ol man came in sayin, 'i don't know
how she got yr number baby, i'm sorry'

lady in brown
no this one is it, 'o baby, ya know i waz high, i'm sorry'

lady in purple
'i'm only human, and inadequacy is what makes us human, &
if we was perfect we wdnt have nothin to strive for, so you
might as well go on and forgive me pretty baby, cause i'm sorry'

lady in green
'shut up bitch, i told you i waz sorry'

lady in orange
no this one is it, 'i do ya like i do ya cause i thot
ya could take it, now i'm sorry'

lady in red
'now i know that ya know i love ya, but i aint ever gonna
love ya like ya want me to love ya, i'm sorry'

lady in blue
one thing i dont need
is any more apologies
i got sorry greetin me at my front door
you can keep yrs
i dont know what to do wit em
they dont open doors
or bring the sun back
they dont make me happy

or get a mornin paper
didnt nobody stop usin my tears to wash cars
cuz a sorry

i am simply tired
of collectin
        i didnt know
        i was so important toyou'
i'm gonna haveta throw some away
i cant get to the clothes in my closet
for alla the sorries
i'm gonna tack a sign to my door
leave a message by the phone
        'if you called
        to say yr sorry
        call somebody
        else
        i dont use em anymore'
i let sorry/ didnt meanta/ & how cd i know abt that
take a walk down a dark & musty street in brooklyn
i'm gonna do exactly what i want to
& i wont be sorry for none of it
letta sorry soothe yr soul/ i'm gonna soothe mine

you were always inconsistent
doin somethin & then bein sorry
beatin my heart to death
talkin bout you sorry

well
i will not call
i'm not goin to be nice
i will raise my voice
& scream & holler
& break things & race the engine
& tell all yr secrets bout yrself to yr face
& i will list in detail everyone of my wonderful lovers
& their ways
i will play oliver lake
loud
& i wont be sorry for none of it

i loved you on purpose
i was open on purpose
i still crave vulnerability & close talk
& i'm not even sorry bout you bein sorry
you can carry all the guilt & grime ya wanna
just dont give it to me
i cant use another sorry
next time
you should admit
you're mean/ low-down/ triflin/ & no count straight out
steada bein sorry alla the time
enjoy bein yrself

lady in red

there waz no air/ the sheets made ripples under his
body like crumpled paper napkins in a summer park/ & lil
specks of somethin from tween his toes or the biscuits
from the day before ran in the sweat that tucked the sheet
into his limbs like he waz an ol frozen bundle of chicken/
& he'd get up to make coffee, drink wine, drink water/ he
wished one of his friends who knew where he waz wd come by
with some blow or some shit/ anythin/ there waz no air/
he'd see the spotlights in the alleyways downstairs movin
in the air/ cross his wall over his face/ & get under the
covers & wait for an all clear or til he cd hear traffic
again/

there waznt nothin wrong with him/ there waznt nothin wrong
with him/ he kept tellin crystal/
any niggah wanna kill vietnamese children more n stay home
& raise his own is sicker than a rabid dog/
that's how their thing had been goin since he got back/
crystal just got inta sayin whatta fool niggah beau waz
& always had been/ didnt he go all over uptown sayin the
child waznt his/ waz some no counts bastard/ & any ol city
police cd come & get him if they wanted/ cuz as soon as
the blood type & shit waz together/ everybody wd know that
crystal waz a no good lyin whore/ and this after she'd been
his girl since she waz thirteen/ when he caught her
on the stairway/

he came home crazy as hell/ he tried to get veterans benefits

to go to school & they kept right on puttin him in
remedial classes/ he cdnt read wortha damn/ so beau
cused the teachers of holdin him back & got himself
a gypsy cab to drive/ but his cab kept breakin
down/ & the cops was always messin wit him/ plus not
gettin much bread/

& crystal went & got pregnant again/ beau most beat
her to death when she tol him/ she still gotta scar
under her right tit where he cut her up/ still crystal
went right on & had the baby/ so now beau willie had
two children/ a little girl/ naomi kenya & a boy/ kwame beau
willie brown/ & there waz no air/

how in the hell did he get in this mess anyway/ somebody
went & tol crystal that beau waz spendin alla his money
on the bartendin bitch down at the merry-go-round cafe/
beau sat straight up in the bed/ wrapped up in the sheets
lookin like john the baptist or a huge baby wit stubble
& nuts/ now he hadta get alla that shit outta crystal's
mind/ so she wd let him come home/ crystal had gone &
got a court order saying beau willie brown had no access
to his children/ if he showed his face he waz subject
to arrest/ shit/ she'd been in his ass to marry her
since she waz 14 years old & here when she 22/ she wanna
throw him out cuz he say he'll marry her/ she burst
out laughin/ hollerin whatchu wanna marry me for now/
so i can support yr

ass/ or come sit wit ya when they lock yr behind
up/ cause they gonna come for ya/ ya goddamn lunatic/
they gonna come/ & i'm not gonna have a thing to do
wit it/ o no i wdnt marry yr pitiful black ass for
nothin & she went on to bed/

the next day beau willie came in blasted & got ta swingin
chairs at crystal/ who cdnt figure out what the hell
he waz doin/ til he got ta shoutin bout how she waz gonna
marry him/ & get some more veterans benefits/ & he cd
stop drivin them crazy spics round/ while they tryin
to kill him for $15/ beau waz sweatin terrible/ beatin
on crystal/ & he cdnt do no more with the table n chairs/
so he went to get the high chair/ & lil kwame waz in it/
& beau waz beatin crystal with the high chair & her son/
& some notion got inta him to stop/ and he run out/

crystal most died/ that's why the police wdnt low
beau near where she lived/ & she'd been tellin the kids
their daddy tried to kill her & kwame/ & he just wanted
to marry her/ that's what/ he wanted to marry her/ &
have a family/ but the bitch waz crazy/ beau willie
waz sittin in this hotel in his drawers drinkin
coffee & wine in the heat of the day spillin shit all
over hisself/ laughin/ bout how he waz gonna get crystal
to take him back/ & let him be a man in the house/ & she
wdnt even have to go to work no more/ he got dressed
all up in his ivory shirt & checkered pants to go see

crystal & get this mess all cleared up/
he knocked on the door to crystal's rooms/ & she
didnt answer/ he beat on the door & crystal & naomi
started cryin/ beau gotta shoutin again how he wanted
to marry her/ & waz she always gonna be a whore/ or
did she wanna husband/ & crystal just kept on
screamin for him to leave us alone/ just leave us
alone/ so beau broke the door down/ crystal held
the children in fronta her/ she picked kwame off the
floor/ in her arms/ & she held naomi by her shoulders/
& kept on sayin/ beau willie brown/ get outta here/
the police is gonna come for ya/ ya fool/ get outta here/
do you want the children to see you act the fool again/
you want kwame to brain damage from you throwin him
round/ niggah/ get outta here/ get out & dont show yr
ass again or i'll kill ya/ i swear i'll kill ya/
he reached for naomi/ crystal grabbed the lil girl &
stared at beau willie like he waz a leper or somethin/
dont you touch my children/ muthafucker/ or i'll kill
you/

beau willie jumped back all humble & apologetic/ i'm
sorry/ i dont wanna hurt em/ i just wanna hold em &
get on my way/ i dont wanna cuz you no more trouble/
i wanted to marry you & give ya things
what you gonna give/ a broken jaw/ niggah get outta here/
he ignored crystal's outburst & sat down motionin for
naomi to come to him/ she smiled back at her daddy/

58

crystal felt naomi givin in & held her tighter/
naomi/ pushed away & ran to her daddy/ cryin/ daddy, daddy
come back daddy/ come back/ but be nice to mommy/
cause mommy loves you/ and ya gotta be nice/
he sat her on his knee/ & played with her ribbons &
they counted fingers & toes/ every so often he
looked over to crystal holdin kwame/ like a statue/
& he'd say/ see crystal/ i can be a good father/
now let me see my son/ & she didnt move/ &
he coaxed her & he coaxed her/ tol her she waz
still a hot lil ol thing & pretty & strong/ didnt
she get right up after that lil ol fight they had
& go back to work/ beau willie oozed kindness &
crystal who had known so lil/ let beau hold kwame/

as soon as crystal let the baby outta her arms/ beau
jumped up a laughin & a gigglin/ a hootin & a hollerin/
awright bitch/ awright bitch/ you gonna marry me/
you gonna marry me . . .
i aint gonna marry ya/ i aint ever gonna marry ya/
for nothin/ you gonna be in the jail/ you gonna be
under the jail for this/ now gimme my kids/ ya give
me back my kids/

he kicked the screen outta the window/ & held the kids
offa the sill/ you gonna marry me/ yeh, i'll marry ya/
anything/ but bring the children back in the house/
he looked from where the kids were hangin from the

fifth story/ at alla the people screamin at him/ &
he started sweatin again/ say to alla the neighbors/
you gonna marry me/

i stood by beau in the window/ with naomi reachin
for me/ & kwame screamin mommy mommy from the fifth
story/ but i cd only whisper/ & he dropped em

    lady in red
i waz missin somethin

    lady in purple
somethin so important

    lady in orange
somethin promised

    lady in blue
a layin on of hands

    lady in green
fingers near my forehead

    lady in yellow
strong

    lady in green
cool

    lady in orange
movin

    lady in purple
makin me whole

    lady in orange
sense

    lady in green
pure

    lady in blue
all the gods comin into me
layin me open to myself

    lady in red
i waz missin somethin

    lady in green
somethin promised

lady in orange
somethin free

lady in purple
a layin on of hands

lady in blue
i know bout/ layin on bodies/ layin outta man
bringin him alla my fleshy self & some of my pleasure
bein taken full eager wet like i get sometimes
i waz missin somethin

lady in purple
a layin on of hands

lady in blue
not a man

lady in yellow
layin on

lady in purple
not my mama/ holdin me tight/ sayin
i'm always gonna be her girl
not a layin on of bosom & womb
a layin on of hands
the holiness of myself released

lady in red
i sat up one nite walkin a boardin house
screamin/ cryin/ the ghost of another woman
who waz missin what i waz missin
i wanted to jump up outta my bones
& be done wit myself
leave me alone
& go on in the wind
it waz too much
i fell into a numbness
til the only tree i cd see
took me up in her branches
held me in the breeze
made me dawn dew
that chill at daybreak
the sun wrapped me up swingin rose light everywhere
the sky laid over me like a million men
i waz cold/ i waz burnin up/ a child
& endlessly weavin garments for the moon
wit my tears

i found god in myself
& i loved her/ i loved her fiercely

> *All of the ladies repeat to them-
> selves softly the lines 'i found god
> in myself & i loved her.' It soon
> becomes a song of joy, started by*

the lady in blue. The ladies sing
first to each other, then gradually
to the audience. After the song
peaks the ladies enter into a closed
tight circle.

lady in brown
& this is for colored girls who have considered
suicide/ but are movin to the ends of their own
rainbows

spell #7:

geechee jibara quik
magic trance manual for
technologically stressed
third world people

foreword/

unrecovered losses/black theater traditions

as a poet in american theater/ i find most activity that takes place on our stages
overwhelmingly shallow/ stilted & imitative. that is probably one of the reasons i insist on
calling myself a poet or writer/ rather than a playwright/ i am interested solely in the poetry
of a moment/ the emotional & aesthetic impact of a character or a line. for too long now afro-
americans in theater have been duped by the same artificial aesthetics that plague our white
counterparts/ "the perfect play," as we know it to be/ a truly european framework for
european psychology/ cannot function efficiently for those of us from this hemisphere.

furthermore/ with the advent of at least 6 musicals about the lives of black musicians &
singers/ (EUBIE, BUBBLING BROWN SUGAR, AIN'T MISBEHAVIN', MAHALIA, etc.)/ the
lives of millions of black people who dont sing & dance for a living/ are left unattended to in
our theatrical literature. not that the lives of Eubie Blake or Fats Waller are well served in
productions lacking any significant book/ but if the lives of our geniuses arent artfully ren-
dered/ & the lives of our regular & precious are ignored/we have a double loss to reckon with.

if we are drawn for a number of reasons/ to the lives & times of black people who
conquered their environments/ or at least their pain with their art, & if these people are
mostly musicians & singers & dancers/ then what is a writer to do to draw the most human &
revealing moments from lives spent in nonverbal activity. first of all we should reconsider
our choices/ we are centering ourselves around these artists for what reasons/because their
lives were richer than ours/ because they did something white people are still having a hard
time duplicating/ because they proved something to the world like Jesse Owens did/ like
Billie Holiday did. i think/ all the above cntributes to the proliferation of musicals abt our
musicians/ without forcing us to confront the real implications of the dynamic itself. we are
compelled to examine these giants in order to give ourselves what we think they gave the
worlds they lived in/ which is an independently created afro-american aesthetic. but we are
going abt this process backwards/ by isolating the art forms & assuming a very narrow
perspective vis-à-vis our own history.

if Fats Waller & Eubie Blake & Charlie Parker & Savilla Fort & Katherine Dunham moved
the world outta their way/ how did they do it/certainly not by mimicking the weakest area in
american art/ the american theater. we must move our theater into the drama of our lives/
which is what the artists we keep resurrecting (or allowing others to resurrect) did in the first
place/ the music & dance of our renowned predecessors appeals to us because it directly
related to lives of those then living & the lives of the art forms.

in other words/ we are selling ourselves & our legacy quite cheaply/since we are trying to
make our primary statements with somebody else's life/ and somebody else's idea of what
theater is. i wd suggest that: we demolish the notion of straight theater for a decade or so, refuse
to allow playwrights to work without dancers & musicians. "coon shows" were somebody
else's idea. we have integrated the notion that a drama must be words/ with no music & no
dance/ cuz that wd take away the seriousness of the event/ cuz we all remember too well/ the
chuckles & scoffs at the notion that all niggers cd sing & dance/ & most of us can sing & dance/
& the reason that so many plays written to silence & stasis fail/ is cuz most black people have

67

a blk child who knew that no black people conducted themselves like amos n andy/ she waz not a blk child who knew that blk children didnt wear tiger skins n chase lions around trees n then eat pancakes/ she waznt a blk child who spoke an english that had evolved naturally/ only to hear a white man's version of blk speech that waz entirely made up & based on no linguistic system besides the language of racism. the man who thought i wrote with intentions of outdoing the white man in the acrobatic distortions of english waz absolutely correct. i cant count the number of times i have viscerally wanted to attack deform n maim the language that i waz taught to hate myself in/ the language that perpetuates the notions that cause pain to every black child as he/she learns to speak of the world & the "self." yes/ being an afro-american writer is something to be self-conscious abt/ & yes/ in order to think n communicate the thoughts n feelings i want to think n communicate/ i haveta fix my tool to my needs/ i have to take it apart to the bone/ so that the malignancies/ fall away/ leaving us space to literally create our own image.

i have not ceased to be amazed when i hear members of an audience whispering to one another in the foyers of theaters/ that they had never imagined they cd feel so much for characters/ even though they were black (or colored/ or niggers, if they don't notice me eavesdropping). on the other hand/ i hear other members of an audience say that there were so many things in the piece that they had felt/ experienced/ but had never found words to express/ even privately/ to themselves. these two phenomena point to the same dilemma/ the straightjacket that the english language slips over the minds of all americans. there are some thoughts that black people just dont have/ according to popular mythology/ so white people never "imagine" we are having them/ & black people "block" vocabularies we perceive to be white folks' ideas.* this will never do. for in addition to the obvious stress of racism n poverty/ afro-american culture/ in attempts to carry on/ to move forward/ has minimized its "emotional" vocabulary to the extent that admitting feelings of rage, defeat, frustration is virtually impossible outside a collective voice. so we can add self-inflicted repression to the cultural causes of our cultural disease of high blood pressure.

in everything i have ever written & everything i hope to write/ i have made use of what Frantz Fanon called "combat breath." although Fanon waz referring to francophone colonies, the schema he draws is sadly familiar:

> there is no occupation of territory, on the one hand and independence of persons on the other. It is the country as a whole, its history, its daily pulsation that are contested, disfigured, in the hope of final destruction. Under this condition, the individual's breathing is an observed, an occupied breathing. It is a combat breathing.†

Fanon goes on to say that "combat breathing" is the living response/ the drive to reconcile the irreconcilable/ the black & white of what we live n where. (unfortunately, this language doesnt allow me to broaden 'black' & "white" to figurative terms/ which is criminal since the words are so much larger n richer than our culture allows.) i have lived with this for 31 years/ as my people have lived with cut-off lives n limbs. spell # 7 is the throes of pain n sensation experienced by my characters responding to the involuntary constriction n amputations of their humanity/ in the context of combat breathing.

it was excruciating to write/ for i had to confront/ again & again/ those moments that had left me with little more than fury n homicidal desires. i included a prologue of a minstrel show/ which made me cry the first times i danced in it/ for the same reasons i had included it. the minstrel may be "banned" as racist/ but the minstrel is more powerful in his deformities than our alleged rejection of him/ for every night we wd be grandly applauded. immediately thereafter/ we began to unveil the "minstrels," who turned out to be as fun-loving as fay:

> please/ let me join you/ i come all the way from brooklyn/ to have a good time/ ya dont think i'm high do ya/ cd i please join ya/ i just wanna have a good old time.

as contorted as sue-jean:

> & i lay in the corner laughin/ with my drawers/ twisted round my ankles & my hair standin every which way/ i waz laughin/ knowin i wd have this child/ myself/ & no one wd ever

*Just examine *Drylongso* by John Langston Gwaltney, Random House, 1980.
†Frantz Fanon, *A Dying Colonialism*, Grove Press, 1967.

68

Fanon goes on to say that "combat breathing" is the living response/ the drive to reconcile the irreconcilable/the black & white of what we live n where. (unfortunately, this language doesnt allow me to broaden "black" & "white" to figurative terms/ which is criminal since the words are so much larger n richer than our culture allows.) i have lived with this for 31 years/ as my people have lived with cut-off lives n limbs. *spell # 7* is the throes of pain n sensation experienced by my characters responding to the involuntary constriction n amputations of their humanity/ in the context of combat breathing.

it was excruciating to write/ for i had to confront/ again & again/ those moments that had left me with little more than fury n homicidal desires. i included a prologue of a minstrel show/ which made me cry the first times i danced in it/ for the same reasons i had included it. the minstrel may be "banned" as racist/ but the minstrel is more powerful in his deformities than our alleged rejection of him/ for every night we wd be grandly applauded. immediately thereafter/ we began to unveil the "minstrels," who turned out to be as fun-loving as fay:

> *please/ let me join you/ i come all the way from brooklyn/ to have a good time/ ya dont think i'm high do ya/ cd i please join ya/ i just wanna have a good old time.*

as contorted as sue-jean:

> *& i lay in the corner laughin/ with my drawers/ twisted round my ankles & my hair standin every which way/ i waz laughin/ knowin i wd have this child/ myself/ & no one wd ever claim him/ cept me/ cuz i was a low-down thing/ layin in sawdust & whiskey stains/ i laughed & had a good time masturbatin in the shadows.*

as angry as the actor who confides:

> *i just want to find out why no one has even been able to sound a gong & all the reporters recite that the gong is ringin/ while we watch all the white people/ immigrants & invaders/ conquistadors & relatives of london debtors from georgia/ kneel & apologize to us/ just for three or four minutes. now/ this is not impossible.*

& after all that/ our true visions & rigors laid bare/ down from the ceiling comes the huge minstrel face/ laughing at all of us for having been so game/ we believed we cd escape his powers/ how naive cd we be/ the magician explains:

> *crackers are born with the right to be alive/*
> *i'm making ours up right here in yr face.*

the most frequently overheard comment abt *spell #7* when it first opened at the public theater/ waz that it was too intense. the cast & i usedta laugh. if this one hour n 45 minutes waz too much/ how in the world did these same people imagine the rest of our lives were/ & wd they ever be able to handle that/ simply being alive & black & feeling in this strange deceitful country.

3/2/80 NYC

Characters

LOU, *a practising magician*
ALEC, *a frustrated, angry actor's actor*
DAHLIA, *young gypsy (singer/dancer)*
ELI, *a bartender who is also a poet*
BETTINA, *Dahlia's co-worker in a chorus*
LILLY, *an unemployed actress working as a
    barmaid*
NATALIE, *a not too successful performer*
ROSS, *guitarist-singer with Natalie*
MAXINE, *an experienced actress*

Spell #7 was first presented by Joseph Papp's Public Theater, New York, in 1979, with the following cast:

Mary Alice
Avery Brooks
Laurie Carlos
Dyane Harvey
Larry Marshall
Reyno
La Tanya Richardson
Beth Shorter
Ellis Williams
Jay Fernandez
Samuel L. Jackson
Jack Landrón

Directed by Oz Scott
Choreographed by Dianne McIntyre
Music by David Murray, Butch Morris
Scenery by Robert Yodice
Costumes by Grace Williams
Lighting by Victor En Yu Tan

Spell #7 was given its British premiere by the Women's Playhouse Trust at the Donmar Theatre, London, on 27 March 1985, in a production directed by Sue Parrish.

70

ACT I

(there is a huge black-face mask hanging from the ceiling of the theater as the audience enters. in a way the show has already begun. for the members of the audience must integrate this grotesque, larger than life misrepresentation of life into their pre-show chatter. slowly the house lights fade, but the mask looms even larger in the darkness.

once the mask is all that can be seen, lou, the magician, enters. he is dressed in the traditional costume of Mr. Interlocutor: tuxedo, bow-tie, top hat festooned with all kinds of whatnots that are obviously meant for good luck. he does a few catchy "soft-shoe" steps & begins singing a traditional version of a black play song)

lou (singing)
10 lil picaninnies all in bed
one fell out and the other nine said:
i sees yr hiney
all black & shiny
i see yr hiney
all black & shiny/ shiny

(as a greeting)

yes/ yes/ yes   isnt life wonderful

(confidentially)

my father is a retired magician
which accounts for my irregular behavior
everything comes outta magic hats
or bottles wit no bottoms & parakeets
are as easy to get as a couple a rabbits
or 3 fifty-cent pieces/ 1958
my daddy retired from magic & took
up another trade cuz this friend a mine
from the 3rd grade/ asked to be made white
on the spot

what cd any self-respectin colored american magician
do wit such an outlandish request/ cept
put all them razzamatazz hocus pocus zippity-doo-dah
thingamajigs away   cuz
colored chirren believin in magic

71

waz becomin politically dangerous for the race
& waznt nobody gonna be made white
on the spot just
from a clap of my daddy's hands
& the reason i'm so peculiar's
cuz i been studyin up on my daddy's technique
& everything i do is magic these days
& it's very colored/ very now you see it/ now you
dont mess wit me •

(boastfully)

                                    i come from a family of retired
sorcerers/ active houngans & pennyante fortune tellers
wit 41 million spirits/ critturs & celestial bodies
on our side
                        i'll listen to yr problems
                        help wit yr career/ yr lover/ yr wanderin spouse
                        make yr grandma's stay in heaven more
                        gratifyin
                        ease yr mother thru menopause & show yr son
                        how to clean his room

*(while lou has been easing the audience into acceptance of his appearance & the
mask (his father, the ancestors, our magic), the rest of the company enters in tattered
fieldhand garb, blackface, and the countenance of stepan fetchit when he waz
frightened. their presence belies the magician's promise that "you'll be colored n love
it," just as the minstrel shows were lies, but lou continues)*

YES YES YES 3 wishes is all you get
    scarlet ribbons for yr hair
    a farm in mississippi
    someone to love you madly
all things are possible
but aint no colored magician in his right mind
gonna make you   white
i mean
        this is blk magic
you lookin at
& i'm fixin yor up good/ fixin you up good & colored
& you gonna be colored all yr life
& you gonna love it/ bein colored/ all yr life/ colored & love it
love it/ bein colored. SPELL #7!

72

(lou claps his hands, & the company which had been absolutely still til this moment/ jumps up. with a rhythm set on a washboard carried by one of them/ they begin a series of steps that identify every period of afro-american entertainment: from acrobats, comedians, tap-dancers, calindy dancers, cotton club choruses, apollo theatre du-wop groups, til they reach a frenzy in the midst of "hambone, hambone where ya been"/ & then take a bow à la bert williams/ the lights bump up abruptly.

the magician, lou, walks thru the black-faced figures in their kneeling poses, arms outstretched as if they were going to sing "mammy." he speaks now [as a companion of the mask] to the same audience who fell so easily into his hands & who were so aroused by the way the black-faced figures "sang n-danced")

lou
why dont you go on & integrate a german-american school in st. louis mo./ 1955/ better yet why dont ya go on & be a red niggah in a blk school in 1954/ i got it/ try & make one friend at camp in the ozarks in 1957/ crawl thru one a jesse james' caves wit a class of white kids waitin outside to see the whites of yr eyes/ why dontcha invade a clique of working class italians trying to be protestant in a jewish community/ & come up a spade/ be a lil too dark/ lips a lil too full/ hair entirely too nappy/ to be beautiful/ be a smart child trying to be dumb/ you go meet somebody who wants/ always/ a lil less/ be cool when yr body says hot/ & more/ be a mistake in racial integrity/ an error in white folks' most absurd fantasies/ be a blk kid in 1954/ who's not blk enuf to lovingly ignore/ not beautiful enuf to leave alone/ not smart enuf to move outta the way/ not bitter enuf to die at an early age/ why dontchu c'mon & live my life for me/ since the dreams aint enuf/ go on & live my life for me/ i didnt want certain moments at all/ i'd give em to anybody . . . awright. alec.

(the black-faced alec gives his minstrel mask to lou when he hears his name/ alec rises. the rest of the company is intimidated by this figure daring to talk without the protection of black-face. they move away from him/ or move in place as if in mourning)

alec
st. louis/ such a colored town/ a whiskey black space of history & neighborhood/ forever ours to lawrenceville/ where the only road open to me waz cleared by colonial slaves/ whose children never moved/ never seems like mended the torments of the Depression or the stains of demented spittle/ dropped from the lips of crystal women/ still makin independence flags/
st. louis/ on a halloween's eve to the veiled prophet/ usurpin the mystery of mardi gras/ i made it mine tho the queen waz always fair/ that

73

parade of pagan floats & tambourines/ commemorates me/ unlike the
lonely walks wit liberal trick or treaters/ back to my front door/ bag half
empty/
 my face enuf to scare anyone i passed/ gee/ a colored kid/ whatta gas.
here/ a tree/ wanderin the horizon/ dipped in blues/ untended bones/
usedta hugs drawls rhythm & decency here a tree/ waitin to be hanged
 sumner high school/ squat & pale on the corner/ like our vision waz to
be vague/ our memory of the war/ that made us free/ to be forgotten/
becomin paler/ linear movement from sous' carolina to missouri/
freedmen/ landin in jackie wilson's yelp/ daughters of the manumitted
swimmin in tina turner's grinds/ this is chuck berry's town disavowin
miscega-nation/ in any situation/ & they let us be/ electric blues & bo
didley/ the rockin pneumonia & boogie-woogie flu/ the slop & short fried
heads/ runnin always to the river chambersburg/ lil italy/ i passed
everyday at the sweet shoppe/ & waz afraid/ the cops raided truants/
regularly/ & after dark i wd not be seen wit any other colored/ sane &
lovin my life

(shouts n cries that are those of a white mob are heard, very loud . . . the still black-
faced figures try to move away from the menacing voices & memories)

voices
hey niggah/ over here

alec
behind the truck lay five hands claspin chains

voices
hey niggah/ over here

alec
round the trees/ 4 more sucklin steel

voices
hey niggah/ over here

alec
this is the borderline

voices
hey niggah/ over here

alec
a territorial dispute

74

voices
hey niggah/ over here

alec (crouched on floor)
cars loaded with families/ fellas from the factory/
one or two practical nurses/ become our trenches/
some dig into cement wit elbows/ under engines/
do not be seen in yr hometown
after sunset/ we suck up our shadows

(finally moved to tear off their "shadows," all but two of the company leave with
their true faces bared to the audience. dahlia has, as if by some magical cause, shed
not only her mask, but also her hideous overalls & picaninny-buckwheat wig, to
reveal a finely laced unitard/ the body of a modern dancer. she throws her mask to
alec, who tosses it away. dahlia begins a lyrical but pained solo as alec speaks for
them)

alec
we will stand here
our shoulders embrace an enormous spirit
my dreams waddle in my lap
run round to miz bertha's
where lil richard gets his process
run backward to the rosebushes
& a drunk man lyin
down the block to the nuns
in pink habits/ prayin in a pink chapel
my dreams run to meet aunt marie
my dreams haunt me like the little geechee river
our dreams draw blood from old sores
this is our space
we are not movin

(dahlia finishes her movement/ alec is seen reaching for her/ lights out. in the
blackout they exit as lou enters. lights come up on lou who repeats bitterly his
challenge to the audience)

lou
why dontchu go on & live my life for me
i didnt want certain moments at all
i'd give them to anybody

(lou waves his hand commanding the minstrel mask to disappear, which it does. he
signals to his left & again by magic, the lights come up higher revealing the interior of

75

a lower manhattan bar & its bartender, eli, setting up for the night. eli greets lou as he continues to set up tables, chairs, candles, etc., for the night's activities. lou goes over to the jukebox, & plays "we are family" by sister sledge. lou starts to tell us exactly where we are, but eli takes over as characters are liable to do. throughout eli's poem, the other members of the company enter the bar in their street clothes, & doing steps reminiscent of their solos during the minstrel sequence. as each enters, the audience is made aware that these ordinary people are the minstrels. the company continues to dance individually as eli speaks)

this is . . .

eli
MY kingdom.
there shall be no trespassers/ no marauders
no tourists in my land
you nurture these gardens   or   be shot on sight
carelessness & other priorities
are not permitted within these walls
i am mantling an array of strength & beauty
no one shall interfere with this
the construction of myself
my city   my theater
my bar   come to my poems
but understand we speak english carefully
& perfect antillean french
our toilets are disinfected
the plants here sing to me each morning
come to my kitchen my parlor even my bed
i sleep on satin   surrounded by hand made
infants who bring me good luck & warmth
come even to my door
the burglar alarm/ armed guards vault from the east side
if i am in danger   a siren shouts
you are welcome
to my kingdom   my city   my self
but yr presence must not disturb these inhabitants
leave nothing out of place/ push no dust under my rugs
leave not a crack in my wine glasses
no finger prints
clean up after yrself in the bathroom
there are no maids here   no days off
for healing   no insurance policies
for dislocation of the psyche

76

aliens/ foreigners/ are granted resident status
we give them a little green card
as they prove themselves non-injurious
to the joy of my nation
i sustain no intrusions/ no double-entendre romance
no soliciting of sadness   in my life
are those who love me well
the rest are denied their visas . . .
is everyone ready to boogie

*(finally, when eli calls for a boogie, the company does a dance that indicates these
people have worked & played together a long time. as dance ends, the company sits &
chats at the tables & at the bar. this is now a safe haven for these "minstrels" off from
work. here they are free to be themselves, to reveal secrets, fantasies, nightmares, or
hope. it is safe because it is segregated & magic reigns.*

*lili, the waitress, is continually moving abt the bar, taking orders for drinks &
generally staying on top of things)*

alec
gimme a triple bourbon/ & a glass of angel dust
these thursday nite audiences are abt to kill me

(eli goes behind bar to get drinks)

dahlia
why do i drink so much?

bettina, lily, natalie (in unison)
who cares?

dahlia
but i'm an actress. i have to ask myself these questions

lily
that's a good reason to drink

dahlia
no/ i mean the character/ alec, you're a director/ give me some motivation

alec
motivation/ if you didn't drink you wd remember that you're not workin

lily
i wish i cd get just one decent part

77

lou
say as lady macbeth or mother courage

eli
ow the hell is she gonna play lady macbeth and macbeth's a white dude?

lily
ross & natalie/ why are you countin pennies like that?

natalie
we had to wait on our money again

ross
and then we didnt get it

bettina
maybe they think we still accept beads & ribbons

natalie
i had to go around wit my tambourine just to get subway fare

eli
dont worry abt it/ have one on me

natalie
thank you eli

bettina (falling out of her chair)
oh . . .

alec
cut her off eli/ dont give her no more

lily
what's the matter bettina/ is yr show closin?

bettina (gets up, resets chair)
no/ my show is not closin/ but if that director asks me to play it any
blacker/ i'm gonna have to do it in a mammy dress

lou
you know/ countin pennies/ lookin for parts/ breakin tambourines/ we
must be outta our minds for doin this

78

bettina
no we're not outta our minds/ we're just sorta outta our minds

lily
no/ we're not outta our minds/ we've been doing this shit a long time . . .
ross/ captain theophilis conneau/ in *a slaver's logbook/* says that "youths
of both sexes wear rings in the nose and lower lip and stick porcupine
quills thru the cartilage of the ear." ross/ when ringlin' bros. comes to
madison square garden/ dontcha know the white people just go

ross
in their cb radios

dahlia
in their mcdonald's hats

eli
with their save america t-shirts & those chirren who score higher on IQ
tests for the white chirren who speak english

alec
when the hockey games absorb all america's attention in winter/ they go
with their fists clenched & their tongues battering their women who dont
know a puck from a 3-yr-old harness racer

bettina
they go & sweat in fierce anger

ross
these factories

natalie
these middle management positions

ross
make madison square garden

bettina
the temple of the primal scream

(lily gets money from cash register & heads toward jukebox)

lily
oh how they love blood

79

natalie
& how they dont even dress for the occasion/ all inconspicuous & pink

eli
now if willie colon come there

bettina
if/ we say/ the fania all stars gonna be there
in that nasty fantasy of the city council

ross
where the hot dogs are not even hebrew national

lily
and the bread is stale .

ross
even in such a place where dance is an obscure notion

bettina
where one's joy is good cause for a boring chat with the pinkerton guard

dahlia
where the halls lead nowhere

eli
& "back to yr seat/ folks"

lily
when all one's budget for cruisin

lou
one's budget for that special dinner with you know who

lily
the one you wd like to love you

bettina
when yr whole reasonable allowance for leisure activity/
buys you a seat where what's goin on dont matter

dahlia
cuz you so high up/ you might be in seattle

80

lily
even in such a tawdry space

eli
where vorster & his pals wd spit & expect black folks to lick it up

ross (stands on chair)
in such a place i've seen miracles

all
oh yeah/ aw/ ross

ross
the miracles

> *("music for the love of it," by butch morris, comes up on the jukebox/ this is a catchy uptempo rhythm & blues post WW II. as they speak the company does a dance that highlights their ease with one another & their familiarity with "all the new dance steps")*

lily
the commodores

dahlia
muhammad ali

natalie
bob marley

alec
& these folks who upset alla 7th avenue with their glow/
how the gold in their braids is new in this world of hard hats & men with
the grace of wounded buffalo/ how these folks in silk & satin/ in bodies
reekin of good love comin/ these pretty muthafuckahs

dahlia
make this barn

lily
this insult to good taste

bettina
a foray into paradise

81

dahlia, lily, alec, natalie & ross (in unison)
we dress up

bettina, eli, & lou (in unison)
we dress up

dahlia
cuz we got good manners

ross
cd you really ask dr. funkenstein to come all that way & greet him in the
clothes you sweep yr kitchen in?

all
NO!

bettina
cd you say to muhammad ali/ well/ i just didnt have a chance to change/
you see i have a job/ & then i went jogging & well, you know its just
madison square garden

lou
my dear/ you know that wont do

natalie
we honor our guests/ if it costs us all we got

dahlia
when stevie wonder sings/ he don't want us lookin like we ain't got no
common sense/ he wants us to be as lovely as we really are/ so we strut &
reggae

eli
i seen some doing the jump up/ i myself just got happy/ but i'm tellin you
one thing for sure

lily
we fill up where we at

bettina
no police

natalie
no cheap beer

82

dahlia
no nasty smellin bano

ross
no hallways fulla derelicts & hustlers

natalie
gonna interfere wit alla this beauty

alec
if it wasnt for us/ in our latino chic/ our rasta-fare our outer space funk
suits & all the rest i have never seen

bettina
tho my daddy cd tell you bout them fox furs & stacked heels/ the
diamonds & marie antoinette wigs

eli
it's not cuz we got money

natalie
it's not cuz if we had money we wd spend it on luxury

lily
it's just when you gotta audience with the pope/ you look yr best

bettina
when you gonna see the queen of england/ you polish yr nails

natalie
when you gonna see one of them/ & you know who i mean

alec
they gotta really know

bettina
we gotta make em feel

eli
we dont do this for any old body

lou
we're doin this for you

natalie
we dress up

alec
is our way of sayin/ you gettin the very best

dahlia
we cant do less/ we love too much to be stingy

ross
they give us too much to be loved ordinary

lily
we simply have good manners

ross
& an addiction to joy

female cast members (in unison)
WHEE . . .

dahlia
we dress up

male cast members (in unison)
HEY . . .

bettina
we gotta show the world/ we gotta corner on the color

ross
happiness just jumped right outta us/ & we are lookin good

*(everyone in the bar is having so much fun/ that maxine takes on an exaggerated
character as she enters/ in order to bring them to attention. the company freezes, half
in respect/ half in parody)*

maxine
cognac!

*(the company relaxes, goes to tables or the bar. in the meantime, ross has remained in
the spell of the character that maxine had introduced when she came in. he goes over
to maxine who is having a drink/ & begins an improvisation)*

84

she left the front gate open/ not quite knowing she wanted someone to
walk on thru the wrought iron fence/ scrambled in whiskey bottles broken
round old bike spokes/ some nice brown man to wind up in her bed/ she
really didnt know/ the sombrero that enveloped her face was a lil too
much for an april nite on the bowery/ & the silver halter dug out from
summer cookouts near riis beach/ didnt sparkle with the intensity of her
promise to have one good time/ before the children came back from
carolina. brooklyn cd be such a drag. every street cept flatbush & nostrand/
reminiscent of europe during the plague/ seems like nobody but sickness
waz out walkin/ drivels & hypes/ a few youngsters lookin for more than
they cd handle/ & then there waz fay/

(maxine rises, begins acting the story out)

waitin for a cab. anyone of the cars inchin along the boulevard cd see fay
waznt no whore/ just a good clean woman out for the nite/ & tho her left
titty jumped out from under her silver halter/ she didnt notice cuz she
waz lookin for a cab. the dank air fondled her long saggin bosom like a
possible companion/ she felt good. she stuck her tin-ringed hand on her
waist & watched her own ankles dance in the nite. she waz gonna have a
good time tonight/ she waz awright/ a whole lotta woman/ wit that special
brooklyn bottom strut. knowin she waznt comin in til dawn/ fay covered
herself/ sorta/ wit a light kacky jacket that just kept her titties from rompin
in the wind/ & she pulled it closer to her/ the winds waz comin/ from
nowhere jabbin/ & there waznt no cabs/ the winds waz beatin her behind/
whisperin/ gigglin/ you aint goin noplace/ you an ol bitch/ shd be at home
wit ur kids. fay beat off the voices/ & an EBONY-TRUE-TO-YOU cab
climbed the curb to get her. *(as cabdriver)*

hope you aint plannin on stayin in brooklyn/ after 8:00 you dead in
brooklyn. *(as narrator)*

she let her titty shake like she thot her mouth oughtta bubble like/ wd
she take off her panties/ i'd take her anywhere.

maxine (as if in cab)
i'm into havin a good time/ yr arms/ veins burstin/ like you usedta lift
tobacco onto trucks or cut cane/ i want you to be happy/ long as we dont
haveta stay in brooklyn

ross
& she made like she waz gypsy rose lee/ or the hotsy totsy girls in the
carnival round from waycross/ when it waz segregated

85

maxine
what's yr name?

ross
my name is raphael

maxine
oh that's nice

ross
& fay moved where i cd see her out the rear view mirror/ waz tellin me all
bout her children & big eddie who waz away/ while we crossed the
manhattan bridge/ i kept smilin. *(as cabdriver)* where exactly you goin?

maxine
i dont really know. i just want to have a good time. take me where i can
see famous people/ & act bizarre like sinatra at the kennedys/ maybe even
go round & beat up folks like jim brown/ throw somebody offa balcony/
you know/ for a good time

ross
the only place i knew/ i took her/ after i kisst the spaces she'd been layin
open to me. fay had alla her $17 cuz i hadnt charged her nothin/ turned
the meter off/ said it waz wonderful to pick up a lady like her on atlantic
avenue/ i saw nobody but those goddamn whores/ & fay

(maxine moves in to ross & gives him a very long kiss)

now fay waz a gd clean woman/ & she waz burstin with pride &
enthusiasm when she walked into the place where I swore/ all the
actresses & actors hung out

*(the company joins in ross' story; responding to maxine as tho she waz entering their
bar)*

oh yes/ there were actresses in braids & lipstick/ wigs & winged tip
pumps/ fay assumed the posture of someone she'd always admired/ etta
james/ the waitress asked her to leave cuz she waz high/ & fay knew better
than that

maxine *(responding to lily's indication of throwing her out)*
i aint high/ i'm enthusiastic/ and i'm gonna have me a gooooooood/ ol
time

86

ross

she waz all dressed up/ she came all the way from brooklyn/ she must
look high cuz i/ the taxi-man/ well i got her a lil excited/ that waz all/ but
she waz gonna cool out/ cuz she waz gonna meet her friends/ at this place/
yes. she knew that/ & she pushed a bunch of rhododendrum/ outta her
way so she cd get over to that table/ & stood over the man with the biggest
niggah eyes & warmest smellin mouth

maxine

please/ let me join you/ i come all the way from brooklyn/ to have a good
time/ you dont think i'm high do ya/ cd i please join ya/ i just wanna have
a good ol time

ross (as bettina turns away)

the woman sipped chablis & looked out the window hopin to see one of
the bowery drunks fall down somewhere/ fay's voice hoverin/ flirtin wit
hope

lou (turning to face maxine)

why dont you go downstairs & put yr titty in yr shirt/ you cant have no
good time lookin like that/ now go on down & then come up & join us

(bettina & lou rise & move to another table)

ross

fay tried to shove her flesh anywhere/ she took off her hat/ bummed a
kool/ swallowed somebody's cognac/ & sat down/ waitin/ for a gd time

maxine (rises & hugs ross)

aw ross/ when am i gonna get a chance to feel somethin like that/ i got
into this business cuz i wanted to feel things all the time/ & all they want
me to do is put my leg in my face/ smile/ &

lily

you better knock on some wood/ maxine/ at least yr workin

bettina

& at least yr not playin a whore/ if some other woman comes in here &
tells me she's playin a whore/ i think i might kill her

eli

you'd kill her so you cd say/ oh dahlia died & i know all her lines

bettina
aw hush up eli/ dnt you know what i mean?

eli
no miss/ i dont/ are you in the theater?

bettina
mr. bartender/ poet sir/ i am theater

dahlia
well miss theater/ that's a surprise/ especially since you fell all over the
damn stage in the middle of my solo

lily
she did

eli
miss theater herself fell down?

dahlia
yeah/ she cant figure out how to get attention without makin somebody
else look bad

maxine
now dahlia/ it waznt that bad/ i hardly noticed her

dahlia
it waz my solo/ you werent sposed to notice her at all!

bettina
you know dahlia/ i didnt do it on purpose/ i cda hurt myself

dahlia
that wd be unfortunate

bettina
well miss thing with those big ass hips you got/ i dont know why you
think you can do the ballet anyway

   (the company breaks; they're expecting a fight)

   dahlia (crossing to bettina)
i got this

(demonstrates her leg extension)

& alla this

(dahlia turns her back to bettina/ & slaps her own backside. bettina grabs dahlia, turns her around & they begin a series of finger snaps that are a paraphrase of ailey choreography for very dangerous fights. eli comes to break up the impending altercation)

eli
ladies ladies ladies

(eli separates the two)

eli
people keep tellin me to put my feet on the ground
i get mad & scream/ there is no ground
only shit pieces from dogs horses & men who dont live
anywhere/ they tell me think straight & make myself
somethin/ i shout & sigh/ i am a poet/ i write poems
i make words cartwheel & somersault down pages
outta my mouth come visions distilled like bootleg
whiskey/ i am like a radio but i am a channel of my own
i keep sayin i write poems/ & people keep askin me
what do i do/ what in the hell is going on?
people keep tellin me these are hard times/ what are
you gonna be doin ten years from now/
what in the hell do you think/ i am gonna be writin poems
i will have poems inchin up the walls of the lincoln tunnel/
i am gonna feed my children poems on rye bread with horseradish/
i am gonna send my mailman off with a poem for his wagon/
give my doctor a poem for his heart/ i am a poet/
i am not a part-time poet/ i am not a amateur poet/
i dont even know what that person cd be/ whoever that is
authorizing poetry as an avocation/ is a fraud/
put yr own feet on the ground

bettina
i'm sorry eli/ i just dont want to be a gypsy all my life

(the bar returns to normal humming & sipping. the lights change to focus on lily/ who begins to say what's really been on her mind. the rest of the company is not aware of lily's private thoughts. only bettina responds to lily, but as a partner in fantasy, not as a voyeur) *lily (illustrating her words with movement)*

i'm gonna simply brush my hair. rapunzel pull yr tresses back into the
tower. & lady godiva give up horseback riding. i'm gonna alter my social &
professional life dramatically. i will brush 100 strokes in the morning/ 100
strokes midday & 100 strokes before retiring. i will have a very busy
schedule. between the local trains & the express/ i'm gonna brush. i brush
between telephone calls. at the disco i'm gonna brush on the slow songs/ i
dont slow dance with strangers. i'ma brush my hair before making love &
after. i'll brush my hair in taxis. while windowshopping. when i have
visitors over the kitchen table/ i'ma brush. i brush my hair while thinking
abt anything. mostly i think abt how it will be when i get my full heada
hair. like lifting my head in the morning will become a chore. i'll try to
turn my cheek & my hair will weigh me down

*(lily falls to the floor. bettina helps lift her to her knees, then begins to dance & mime
as lily speaks)*

i dream of chaka khan/ chocolate from graham central station with all
seven wigs/ & medusa. i brush & brush. i use olive oil hair food/ &
posner's vitamin E. but mostly i brush & brush. i may lose contact with
most of my friends. i cd lose my job/ but i'm on unemployment & brush
while waiting on line for my check. i'm sure i get good recommendations
from my social worker: such a fastidious woman/ that lily/ always
brushing her hair. nothing in my dreams suggests that hair brushing/ per
se/ has anything to do with my particular heada hair. a therapist might say
that the head fulla hair has to do with something else/ like: a symbol of
lily's unconscious desires. but i have no therapist

*(she takes imaginary pen from bettina, who was pretending to be a therapist & sits
down at table across from her)*

& my dreams mean things to me/ like if you dreamed abt tobias/ then
something has happened to tobias/ or he is gonna show up. if you dream
abt yr grandma who's dead/ then you must be doing something she doesnt
like/ or she wdnta gone to all the trouble to leave heaven like that. if you
dream something red/ you shd stop. if you dream something green/ you
shd keep doing it. if a blue person appears in yr dreams/ then that person
is yr true friend

    & that's how i see my dreams. & this head fulla hair i have in my
dreams is lavender & nappy as a 3-yr-old's in a apple tree. i can fry an egg
& see the white of the egg spreadin in the grease like my hair is gonna
spread in the air/ but i'm not egg-yolk yellow/ i am brown & the egg white

isnt white at all/ it is my actual hair/ & it wd go on & on forever/ irregular
like a rasta-man's hair. irregular/ gargantuan & lavender. nestled on blue
satin pillows/ pillows like the sky. & so i fry my eggs. i buy daisies dyed
lavender & laced lavender tablemats & lavender nail polish. though i
never admit it/ i really do believe in magic/ & can do strange things when
something comes over me. soon everything around me will be lavender/
fluffy & consuming. i will know not a moment of bitterness/ through all
the wrist aching & tennis elbow from brushing/ i'll smile. no regrets/ "je
ne regrette rien" i'll sing like edith piaf. when my friends want me to go
see tina turner or pacheco/ i'll croon "sorry/ i have to brush my hair."
   i'll find ambrosia. my hair'll grow pomegranates & soil/ rich as round
the aswan/ i wake in my bed to bananas/ avocados/ collard greens/ the
tramps' latest disco hit/ fresh croissant/ pouilly fuissé/ ishmael reed's
essays/ charlotte carter's stories/ all stream from my hair.
   & with the bricks that plop from where a 9-year-old's top braid wd be/
i will brush myself a house with running water & a bidet. i'll have a closet
full of clean bed linen & the lil girl from the castro convertible
commercial will come & open the bed repeatedly & stay on as a helper to
brush my hair. lily is the only person i know whose every word leaves a
purple haze on the tip of yr tongue. when this happens i says clouds are
forming/ & i has to close the windows. violet rain is hard to remove from
blue satin pillows

(lou, the magician, gets up. he points to lily sitting very still. he reminds us that it is
only thru him that we are able to know these people without the "masks"/ the lies/ &
he cautions that all their thoughts are not benign. they are not safe from what they
remember or imagine)

lou
you have t come with me/ to this place where magic is/
to hear my song/ some times i forget & leave my tune
in the corner of the closet under all the dirty clothes/
in this place/ magic asks me where i've been/ how i've
been singin/ lately i leave my self in all the wrong hands/
in this place where magic is involved/
undoin our masks/ i am able to smile & answer that.
in this place where magic always asks for me
i discovered a lot of other people who talk without mouths
who listen to what you say/ by watchin yr jewelry dance
& in this place where magic stays
you can let yrself in or out
but when you leave yrself at home/ burglars & daylight thieves
pounce on you & sell yr skin/ at cut-rates on tenth avenue

(ross has been playing the acoustic guitar softly as lou spoke. alec picks up on the
train of lou's thoughts & tells a story that in turn captures natalie's attention. slowly,
natalie becomes the woman alec describes)

alec

she had always wanted a baby/ never a family/ never a man/
she had always wanted a baby/ who wd suckle & sleep
a baby boy who wd wet/ & cry/ & smile
suckle & sleep
when she sat in bars/ on the stool/ near the door/ & cross from the juke
box/ with her legs straddled & revealin red lace pants/ & lil hair smashed
under the stockings/ she wd think how she wanted this baby & how she
wd call the baby/ "myself" & as she thot/ bout this brown lil thing/ she
ordered another bourbon/ double & tilted her head as if to cuddle some
infant/ not present/ the men in the bar never imagined her as someone's
mother/ she rarely tended her own self carefully/

(natalie rises slowly, sits astride on the floor)

just enough to exude a languid sexuality that teased the men off work/ &
the bartender/ ray who waz her only friend/ women didnt take to her/ so
she spent her afternoons with ray/ in the bar round the corner from her lil
house/ that shook winsomely in a hard wind/ surrounded by three weepin
willows

natalie

my name is sue-jean & i grew here/ a ordinary colored girl with no claims
to any thing/ or anyone/ i drink now/ bourbon/ in harder times/ beer/ but i
always wanted to have a baby/ a lil boy/ named myself

alec
one time/ she made it with ray

natalie

& there waz nothin special there/ only a hot rough bangin/ a brusque
barrelin throwin of torso/ legs & sweat/ ray wanted to kiss me/ but i
screamed/ cuz i didnt like kissin/ only fuckin/ & we rolled round/ i waz a
peculiar sorta woman/ wantin no kisses/ no caresses/ just power/ heat & no
easiness of thrust/ ray pulled himself outa me/ with no particular
exclamation/ he smacked me on my behind/ i waz grinnin/ & he took that
as a indication of his skill/ he believed he waz a good lover/ & a woman
like me/ didnt never want nothin but a hard dick/ & everyone believed
that/ tho no one in town really knew

92

alec
so ray/ went on behind the bar cuz he had got his

natalie
& i lay in the corner laughin/ with my drawers/ twisted round my ankles &
my hair standin every which way/ i waz laughin/ knowin i wd have this
child/ myself/ & no one wd ever claim him/ cept me cuz i waz a low-down
thing/ layin in sawdust & whiskey stains/ i laughed & had a good time
masturbatin in the shadows.

alec
sue-jean ate starch for good luck

natalie
like mama kareena/ tol me

alec
& she planted five okras/ five collards/ & five tomatoes

natalie
for good luck too/ i waz gonna have this baby/ i even went over to the
hospital to learn prenatal care/ & i kept myself clean

alec
sue-jean's lanky body got ta spreadin & her stomach waz taut & round
high in her chest/ a high pregnancy is sure to be a boy/ & she smiled

natalie
i stopped goin to the bar

alec
started cannin food

natalie
knittin lil booties

alec
even goin to church wit the late nite radio evangelist

natalie
i gotta prayer cloth for the boy/ myself waz gonna be safe from all that his
mama/ waz prey to

alec

sure/ sue-jean waz a scandal/ but that waz to be expected/ cuz she waz
always a po criterish chile

natalie

& wont no man bout step my way/ ever/ just cuz i hadda bad omen on me/
from the very womb/ i waz bewitched is what the ol women usedta say

alec

sue-jean waz born on a full moon/ the year of the flood/ the night the river
raised her skirts & sat over alla the towns & settlements for 30 miles in
each direction/ the nite the river waz in labor/ gruntin & groanin/ splittin
trees & families/ spillin cupboards over the ground/ waz the nite sue-jean
waz born

natalie

& my mother died/ drownin/ holdin me up over the mud crawlin in her
mouth

alec

somebody took her & she lived to be the town's no one/ now with the boy
achin & dancin in her belly/ sue-jean waz a gay & gracious woman/ she
made pies/ she baked cakes & left them on the stoop of the church she had
never entered just cuz she wanted/ & she grew plants & swept her floors/
she waz someone she had never known/ she waz herself with child/ & she
waz a wonderful bulbous thing

natalie

the nite/ myself waz born/ ol mama kareena from the hills came down to
see bout me/ i hollered & breathed/ i did exactly like mama kareena said/
& i pushed & pushed & there waz a earthquake up in my womb/ i wanted
to sit up & pull the tons of logs trapped in my crotch out/ so i cd sleep/
but it wdnt go way/ i pushed & thot i saw 19 horses runnin in my pussy/ i
waz sure there waz a locomotive stalled up in there burnin coal & steamin
& pushin gainst a mountain

alec

finally the child's head waz within reach & mama kareena/ brought the
boy into this world

natalie

& he waz awright/ with alla his toes & his fingers/ his lil dick & eyes/
elbows that bent/ & legs/ straight/ i wanted a big glassa bourbon/ & mama

kareena brought it/ right away/ we sat drinkin the bourbon/ & lookin at the
child whose name waz myself/ like i had wanted/ & the two of us ate
placenta stew . . . i waznt really sure . . .

alec
sue-jean you werent really sure you wanted myself to wake up/ you
always wanted him to sleep/ or at most to nurse/ the nites yr dreams were
disturbed by his cryin

natalie
i had no one to help me

alec
so you were always with him/ & you didnt mind/ you knew this waz yr
baby/ myself/ & you cuddled him/ carried him all over the house with you
all day/ no matter/ what

natalie
everythin waz going awright til/ myself wanted to crawl

alec (moving closer to natalie)
& discover a world of his own/ then you became despondent/ & yr tits
began to dry & you lost the fullness of yr womb/ where myself/ had lived

natalie
i wanted that back

alec
you wanted back the milk

natalie
& the tight gourd of a stomach i had when myself waz bein in me

alec
so you slit his wrists

natalie
he waz sleepin

alec
sucked the blood back into yrself/ & waited/ myself shriveled up in his
crib

natalie
a dank lil blk thing/ i never touched him again

alec
you were always holdin yr womb/ feelin him kick & sing to you bout love/
& you wd hold yr tit in yr hand

natalie
like i always did when i fed him

alec
& you waited & waited/ for a new myself. tho there were labor pains

natalie
& i screamed in my bed

alec
yr legs pinnin to the air

natalie
spinnin sometimes like a ferris wheel/ i cd get no child to fall from me

alec
& she forgot abt the child bein born/ & waz heavy & full all her life/ with
"myself"

natalie
who'll be out/ any day now

> *(eli moves from behind the bar to help natalie/ or to clean tables. he doesnt really
> know. he stops suddenly)*

eli
aint that a goddamn shame/ aint that a way
to come into the world
sometimes i really cant write
sometimes i cant even talk

> *(the minstrel mask comes down very slowly. blackout, except for lights on the big
> minstrel mask which remains visible throughout intermission)*

96

ACT II

(all players onstage are frozen, except lou, who makes a motion for the big minstrel mask to disappear again. as the mask flies up, lou begins)

lou
in this place where magic stays
you can let yrself in or out

(he makes a magic motion. a samba is heard from the jukebox & activity is begun in the bar again. dahlia, natalie & lily enter, apparently from the ladies room)

natalie
i swear we went to that audition in good faith/ & that man asked us where we learned to speak english so well/ i swear this foreigner/ asked us/ from the city of new york/ where we learned to speak english.

lily
all i did was say "bom dia/ como vai"/ and the englishman got red in the face

lou (as the englishman)
yr from the states/ aren't you?

lily
"sim"/ i said/ in good portuguese

lou
but you speak portuguese

lily
"sim" i said/ in good portuguese

lou
how did you pick that up?

lily
i hadda answer so simple/ i cdnt say i learned it/ cuz niggahs cant learn & that wda been too hard on the man/ so i said/ in good english: i held my ear to the ground & listened to the samba from bêlim

dahlia
you should have said: i make a lotta phone calls to casçais, portugao

97

bettina
i gotta bahiano boyfriend

natalie
how abt: i waz an angolan freedom fighter

maxine
no/ lily/ tell him: i'm a great admirer of zeza motto & leci brandao

lily
when the japanese red army invaded san juan/ they poisoned the papaya
with portuguese. i eat a lotta papaya. last week/ i developed a strange
schizophrenic condition/ with 4 manifest personalities: one spoke english
& understood nothing/ one spoke french & had access to the world/ one
spoke spanish & voted against statehood for puerto rico/ one spoke
portuguese. "eu naõ falo ingles entaõ y voce"/ i dont speak english
anymore/ & you?

   *(all the women in the company have been doing samba steps as the others spoke/ now
   they all dance around a table in their own ritual/ which stirs alec & lou to interrupt
   this female segregation. the women scatter to different tables, leaving the two
   interlopers alone. so, alec & lou begin their conversation)*

alec
not only waz she without a tan, but she held her purse close to her hip
like a new yorker. someone who rode the paris métro or listened to
mariachis in plaza santa cecilia. she waz not from here

   (he sits at table)

lou (following suit)
but from there

alec
some there where coloureds/ mulattoes/ negroes/ blacks cd make a living
big enough to leave there to come here/ where no one went there much
any more for all sorts of reasons

lou
the big reasons being immigration restrictions & unemployment.
nowadays, immigration restrictions of every kind apply to any non-
european persons who want to go there from here

alec

some who want to go there from here risk fetching trouble with the
customs authority there

lou

or later with the police, who can tell who's not from there cuz the shoes
are pointed & laced strange

alec

the pants be for august & yet it's january

lou

the accent is patterned for pétionville, but working in crown heights

alec

what makes a person comfortably ordinary here cd make him dangerously
conspicuous there.

lou

so some go to london or amsterdam or paris/ where they are so abounding
no one tries to tell who is from where

alec

still the far right wing of every there prints lil pamphlets that say
everyone from there shd leave & go back where they came from

lou

this is manifest legally thru immigration restrictions & personally thru
unemployment

alec

anyway the yng woman waz from there/ & she waz alone. that waz good.
cuz if a person had no big brother in gronigen/ no aunt in rouen

lou

no sponsor in chicago

alec

this brown woman from there might be a good idea. everybody in the
world/ european & non-european alike/ everybody knows that rich white
girls are hard to find. some of them joined the weather underground/ some
the baader-meinhof gang.

lou
a whole bunch of them gave up men entirely

alec
so the exotic lover in the sun routine becomes more difficult to swing/ if
she wants to talk abt plastic explosives & the resistance of the black
masses to socialism/ instead of giving head as the tide slips in or lending
money

lou
just for the next few days

alec
is hard to find a rich white girl who is so dumb/ too

lou
anyway. the whole world knows/ european & non-european alike/ the
whole world knows that nobody loves the black woman like they love
farrah fawcett-majors. the whole world dont turn out for a dead black
woman like they did for marilyn monroe.

alec
actually/ the demise of josephine baker waz an international event

lou
but she waz a war hero
the worldwide un-beloved black woman is a good idea/ if she is from
there & one is a young man with gd looks/ piercing eyes/ & knowledge of
several romantic languages

> *(throughout this conversation, alec & lou will make attempts to seduce, cajole, & woo*
> *the women of the bar as their narrative indicates. the women play the roles as*
> *described, being so moved by romance)*

alec
the best dancing spots/ the hill where one can see the entire bay at
twilight

lou
the beach where the seals & pelicans run free/ the hidden "local"
restaurants

100

alec
"aw babee/ you so pretty" begins often in the lobby of hotels where the
bright handsome yng men wd be loiterers

lou
were they not needed to tend the needs of the black women from there

alec
tourists are usually white people or asians who didnt come all this way to
meet a black woman who isnt even foreign

lou
so hotel managers wink an eye at the yng men in the lobby or by the bar
who wd be loitering/ but are gonna help her have a gd time

alec
maybe help themselves too

lou
everybody in the world/ european & non-european alike/ everybody
knows the black woman from there is not treated as a princess/ as a jewel/
a cherished lover

alec
that's not how sapphire got her reputation/ nor how mrs. jefferson
perceives the world

lou
you know/ babee/ you dont act like them. aw babee/ you so pretty

alec
the yng man in the hotel watches the yng blk woman sit & sit & sit/ while
the european tourists dance with each other/ & the dapper local fellas
mambo frenetically with secretaries from arizona/ in search of the missing
rich white girl. our girl sits &

female cast members (in unison)
sits & sits & sits

alec (to dahlia & natalie, who move to the music)
maybe she is courageous & taps her foot. maybe she is bold & enjoys the
music/ smiling/ shaking shoulders. let her sit & let her know she is
unwanted

lou
she is not white & she is not from here

alec
let her know she is not pretty enuf to dance the next merengue. then
appear/ mysteriously/ in the corner of the bar. stare at her. just stare. when
stevie wonder's song/ "isnt she lovely"/ blares thru the red-tinted light/
ask her to dance & hold her as tyrone power wda. hold her & stare

(ross & eli sing the chorus to stevie wonder's "isn't she lovely")

lou
dance yr ass off. she has been discovered by the non-european fred astaire

alec
let her know she is a surprise/ an event. by the look on yr face you've
never seen anyone like this black woman from there. you say: "aw/ you
not from here?"/ totally astonished. she murmurs that she is from there. as
if to apologize for her unfortunate place of birth

lou
you say

alec
aw babee/ you so pretty. & it's all over

lou
a night in a pension near the sorbonne. pick her up from the mattress.
throw her gainst the wall in a show of exotic temper & passion:
"maintenant/ tu es ma femme. nous nous sommes mariés." unions of this
sort are common wherever the yng black women travel alone. a woman
traveling alone is an affront to the non-european man who is known the
world over/ to european & non-european alike/ for his way with women

alec
his sense of romance/ how he can say:

lou
aw babee/ you so pretty . . . and even a beautiful woman will believe no
one else ever recognized her loveliness

eli
or else/ he comes to a cafe in willemstad in the height of the sunset. an
able-bodied/ sinewy yng man who wants to buy one beer for the yng

102

woman. after the first round/ he discovers he has run out of money/ so she
must buy the next round/ when he discovers/ what beautiful legs you
have/ how yr mouth is like the breath of tiger lilies. we shall make love in
the/ how you call it/ yes in the earth/ in the dirt/ i will have you in my/
how you say/ where things grow/ aw/ yes/ i will have you in the soil.
probably under the stars & smelling of wine/ an unforgettable
international affair can be consummated

(the company sings "tara's theme" as eli ends his speech. eli & bettina take a tango
walk to the bar, while maxine mimics a 1930's photographer, shooting them as they
sail off into the sunset)

maxine
at 11:30 one evening i waz at the port authority/ new york/ united states/
myself. now i waz there & i spoke english & waz holding approximately
$7 american currency/ when a yng man from there came up to me from
the front of the line of people waiting for the princeton new jersey united
states local bus. i mean to say/ he gave up his chance for a good seat to
come say to me:

ross
i never saw a black woman reading nietzsche

maxine
i waz demure enough/ i said i have to for a philosophy class. but as the
night went on i noticed this yng man waz so much like the other yng men
from here/ who use their bodies as bait & their smiles as passport
alternatives. anyway the night did go on. we were snuggled together in the
rear of the bus going down the jersey turnpike. he told me in english/ that
he had spoken all his life in st. louis/ where he waz raised:

ross
i've wanted all my life to meet someone like you. i want you to meet my
family/ who haven't seen me in a long time/ since i left missouri looking
for opportunity . . .

(he is lost for words)

lou (stage whisper)
opportunity to sculpt

ross
thank you/ opportunity to sculpt

103

maxine
he had been everyplace/ he said

ross
you arent like any black woman i've ever met anywhere

maxine
here or there

ross
i had to come back to new york cuz of immigration restrictions & high unemployment among black american sculptors abroad

maxine
just as we got to princeton/ he picked my face up from his shoulder & said:

ross
aw babee/ you so pretty

maxine
aw babee/ you so pretty. i believe that night i must have looked beautiful for a black woman from there/ though i cd be asked at any moment to tour the universe/ to climb a 6-story walkup with a brilliant & starving painter/ to share kadushi/ to meet mama/ to getta kiss each time the swing falls toward the willow branch/ to imagine where he say he from/ & more. i cd/ i cd have all of it/ but i cd not be taken/ long as i don't let a stranger be the first to say:

lou
aw babee/ you so pretty

maxine
after all/ immigration restrictions & unemployment cd drive a man to drink or to lie

(she breaks away from ross)

so if you know yr beautiful & bright & cherishable awready/ when he say/ in whatever language:

alec (to natalie)
aw babee/ you so pretty

104

maxine
you cd say:

natalie
i know. thank you

maxine
then he'll smile/ & you'll smile. he'll say:

eli (stroking bettina's thigh)
what nice legs you have

maxine
you can say:

bettina (removing his hand)
yes. they run in the family

maxine
oh! whatta universe of beautiful & well traveled women!

male cast members (in unison)
aw babee/ i've never met anyone like you

female cast members (in unison, pulling away from men to stage edges)
that's strange/ there are millions of us!

(men all cluster after unsuccessful attempts to persuade their women to talk. alec gets the idea to serenade the women; ross takes the first verse, with men singing back-up. song is "ooh baby," by smokey robinson)

ross (singing)
i did you wrong/ my heart went out to play/ but in the game
i lost you/ what a price to pay/ i'm cryin . . .

male players (singing)
oo oo oo/ baby baby. . . . oo oo oo/ baby baby

(this brings no response from the women; the men elect eli to lead the second verse)

eli
mistakes i know i've made a few/ but i'm only human

105

you've made mistakes too/ i'm cryin . . .
oo oo oo/ baby baby . . . oo oo oo/ baby baby

(the women slowly forsake their staunch indignation/ returning to the arms of their
partners. all that is except lily, who walks abt the room of couples awkwardly)

male cast members & lily (singing)
i'm just about at the end of my rope
but i can't stop trying/ i cant give up hope
cause i/ i believe one day/ i'll hold you near
whisper i love you/ until that day is here
i'm cryin . . . oo oo oo/ baby baby

(lily begins as the company continues to sing)

lily
unfortunately
the most beautiful man in the world
is unavailable
    that's what he told me
i saw him wandering abt/ said well this is one of a kind
& i might be able to help him out
so alone & pretty in all this ganja & bodies melting
he danced with me & i cd become that
a certain way to be held that's considered in advance
a way a thoughtful man wd kiss a woman who
cd be offended easily/ but waznt cuz
of course the most beautiful man in the world
knows exactly what to do
with someone who knows that's who he is/
these dreads fallin thru my dress
so my nipples just stood up
these hands playin the guitar on my back
the lips somewhere between my neck
& my forehead
talking bout ocho rios & how i really must go
marcus garvey cda come in the door & we/
we wd still be dancin that dance
the motion that has more to do with kinetic energy
than shootin stars/ more to do with the impossibility
of all this/ & how it waz awready bein too much
our reason failed
we tried to go away & be just together

106

aside from the silence that weeped
with greed/ we didnt need/ anything/ but one another
for tonite
but he is the most beautiful man in the world
    says he's unavailable/
& this man whose eyes made me
half-naked & still & brazen/ was singin with me
since we cd not talk/ we sang

(male players end their chorus with a flourish)

    lily
we sang with bob marley
this man/ surely the most beautiful man in the world/ & i
sang/ "i wanna love you & treat you right/

(the couples begin different kinds of reggae dances)

i wanna love you every day & every nite"

    the company (dancing & singing)
we'll be together with the roof right over our heads
we'll share the shelter of my single bed
we'll share the same room/ jah provide the bread

    dahlia (stops dancing during conversation)
i tell you it's not just the part that makes me love you so much

    lou
what is it/ wait/ i know/ you like my legs

    dahlia
yes/ uh huh/ yr legs & yr arms/ & . . .

    lou
but that's just my body/ you started off saying you loved me & now i see
it's just my body

    dahlia
oh/ i didnt mean that/ it's just i dont know you/ except as the character
i'm sposed to love/ & well i know rehearsal is over/ but i'm still in love
with you

(they go to the bar to get drinks, then sit at a table)

ross
but baby/ you have to go on the road. we need the money

natalie
i'm not going on the road so you can fuck all these aspiring actresses

ross
aw/ just some of them/ baby

natalie
that's why i'm not going

ross
if you dont go on the road i'll still be fuckin em/ but you & me/ we'll be in
trouble/ you understand?

natalie (stops dancing)
no i dont understand

ross
well let me break it down to you

natalie
please/ break it down to me

bettina (stops dancing)
hey/ natalie/ why dont you make him go on the rcad/ they always want us
to be so goddamned conscientious

alec (stops dancing)
dont you think you shd mind yr own bizness?

natalie
yeah bettina/ mind yr own bizness

(she pulls ross to a table with her)

bettina (to alec)
no/ i'm tired of having to take any & every old job to support us/ & you get
to have artistic integrity & refuse parts that are beneath you

alec
thats right/ i'm not playing the fool or the black buck pimp circus/ i'm an

actor not a stereotype/ i've been trained. you know i'm a classically
trained actor

   bettina
& just what do you think we are?

   maxine
well/ i got offered another whore part downtown

   eli
you gonna take it?

   maxine
yeah

   lily
if you dont/ i know someone who will

   alec (to bettina)
i told you/ we arent gonna get anyplace/ by doin every bit part for a
niggah that someone waves in fronta my face

   bettina
& we arent gonna live long on nothin/ either/ cuz i'm quittin my job

   alec
be in the real world for once & try to understand me

   bettina
you mean/ i shd understand that you are the great artist & i'm the trouper.

   alec
i'm not sayin that we cant be gigglin & laughin all the time dancin
around/ but i cant stay in these "hate whitey" shows/ cuz they arent true

   bettina
a failure of imagination on yr part/ i take it

   alec
no/ an insult to my person

   bettina
oh i see/ you wanna give the people some more make-believe

109

alec
i cd always black up again & do minstrel work/ wd that make you happy?

bettina
there is nothin niggardly abt a decent job. work is honorable/ work!

alec
well/ i got a problem. i got lots of problems/ but i got one i want you to fix
& if you can fix it/ i'll do anything you say. last spring this niggah from
the midwest asked for president carter to say he waz sorry for that
forgettable phenomenon/ slavery/ which brought us all together. i never
did get it/ none of us ever got no apology from no white folks abt not bein
considered human beings/ that makes me mad & tired. someone told me
"roots" was the way white folks worked out their guilt/ the success of
"roots" is the way white folks assuaged their consciences/ i dont know
this/ this is what i waz told. i dont get any pleasure from nobody watchin
me trying to be a slave i once waz/ who got away/ when we all know they
had an emancipation proclamation/ that the civil war waz not fought over
us. we all know that we/ actually dont exist unless we play football or
basketball or baseball or soccer/ pélé/ see they still import a strong niggah
to earn money. art here/ isnt like in the old country/ where we had some
spare time & did what we liked to do/ i dont know this either/ this is also
something i've been told. i just want to find out why no one has even
been able to sound a gong & all the reporters recite that the gong is ringin/
while we watch all the white people/ immigrants & invaders/
conquistadors & relatives of london debtors from georgia/ kneel &
apologize to us/ just for three or four minutes. now/ this is not impossible/
& someone shd make a day where a few minutes of the pain of our lives is
acknowledged. i have never been very interested in what white people
did/ cuz i waz able/ like most of us/ to have very lil to do with them/ but
if i become a success that means i have to talk to white folks more than in
high school/ they are everywhere/ you know how they talk abt a
neighborhood changin/ we suddenly become all over the place/ they are
now all over my life/ & i dont like it. i am not talkin abt poets & painters/
not abt women & lovers of beauty/ i am talkin abt that proverbial white
person who is usually a man who just/ turns yr body around/ looks at yr
teeth & yr ass/ who feels yr calves & back/ & agrees on a price. we are/ you
see/ now able to sell ourselves/ & i am still a person who is tired/ a person
who is not into his demise/ just three minutes for our lives/ just three
minutes of silence & a gong in st. louis/ oakland/ in los angeles . . .

(the entire company looks at him as if he's crazy/ he tries to leave the bar/ but bettina
stops him)

110

bettina
you're still outta yr mind. ain't no apologies keeping us alive.

lou
what are you gonna do with white folks kneeling all over the country
anyway/ man

(lou signals everyone to kneel)

lily
they say i'm too light to work/ but when i asked him what he meant/ he
said i didnt actually look black. but/ i said/ my mama knows i'm black &
my daddy/ damn sure knows i'm black/ & he is the only one who has a
problem thinkin i'm black/ i said so let me play a white girl/ i'm a
classically trained actress & i need the work & i can do it/ he said that
wdnt be very ethical of him. can you imagine that shit/ not ethical

natalie
as a red-blooded white woman/ i cant allow you all to go on like that

(natalie starts jocularly)

cuz today i'm gonna be a white girl/ i'll retroactively wake myself up/ ah
low & behold/ a white girl in my bed/ but first i'll haveta call a white girl i
know to have some more accurate information/ what's the first thing white
girls think in the morning/ do they get up being glad they aint niggahs/ do
they remember mama/ or worry abt gettin to work/ do they work?/ do they
play isadora & wrap themselves in sheets & go tip toeing to the kitchen to
make maxwell house coffee/ oh i know/ the first thing a white girl does in
the morning is fling her hair/
         so now i'm done with that/ i'm gonna water my plants/ but am i a po
white trash white girl with a old jellyjar/ or am i a sophisticated &
protestant suburbanite with 2 valiums slugged awready & a porcelain
water carrier leading me up the stairs strewn with heads of dolls & nasty
smellin white husband person's underwear/ if i was really protected from
the niggahs/ i might go to early morning mass & pick up a tomato pie on
the way home/ so i cd eat it during the young & the restless. in williams
arizona as a white girl/ i cd push the navaho women outta my way in the
supermarket & push my nose in the air so i wdnt haveta smell them.
coming from bay ridge on the train i cd smile at all the black & puerto
rican people/ & hope they cant tell i want them to go back where they
came from/ or at least be invisible
         i'm still in my kitchen/ so i guess i'll just have to fling my hair again

111

& sit down. i shd pinch my cheeks to bring the color back/ i wonder why the colored lady hasnt arrived to clean my house yet/ so i cd go to the beauty parlor & sit under a sunlamp to get some more color back/ it's terrible how god gave those colored women such clear complexions/ it take em years to develop wrinkles/ but beauty can be bought & flattered into the world.

as a white girl on the street/ i can assume since i am a white girl on the streets/ that everyone notices how beautiful i am/ especially lil black & caribbean boys/ they love to look at me/ i'm exotic/ no one in their families looks like me/ poor things. if i waz one of those white girls who loves one of those grown black fellas/ i cd say with my eyes wide open/ totally sincere/ oh i didnt know that/ i cd say i didnt know/ i cant/ i dont know how/ cuz i'ma white girl & i dont have to do much of anything.

all of this is the fault of the white man's sexism/ oh how i loathe tight-assed thin-lipped pink white men/ even the football players lack a certain relaxed virility. that's why my heroes are either just like my father/ who while he still cdnt speak english knew enough to tell me how the niggers shd go back where they came from/ or my heroes are psychotic faggots who are white/ or else they are/ oh/ you know/ colored men.

being a white girl by dint of my will/ is much more complicated than i thought it wd be/ but i wanted to try it cuz so many men like white girls/ white men/ black men/ latin men/ jewish men/ asians/ everybody. so i thought if i waz a white girl for a day i might understand this better/ after all gertrude stein wanted to know abt the black women/ alice adams wrote *thinking abt billie/* joyce carol oates has three different black characters all with the same name/ i guess cuz we are underdeveloped individuals or cuz we are all the same/ at any rate i'm gonna call this thinkin abt white girls/ cuz helmut newton's awready gotta book called *white women/* see what i mean/ that's a best seller/ one store i passed/ hadda sign said/

> WHITE WOMEN
> SOLD OUT

it's this kinda pressure that forces us white girls to be so absolutely pathological abt the other women in the world/ who now that they're not all servants or peasants want to be considered beautiful too. we simply krinkle our hair/ learn to dance the woogie dances/ slant our eyes with make-up or surgery/ learn spanish & claim argentinian background/ or as a real trump card/ show up looking like a real white girl. you know all western civilization depends on us/

i still havent left my house. i think i'll fling my hair once more/ but this time with a pout/ cuz i think i havent been fair to the sisterhood/

112

women's movement faction of white girls/ although/ they always ask what do you people really want. as if the colored woman of the world were a strange sort of neutered workhorse/ which isnt too far from reality/ since i'm still waiting for my cleaning lady & the lady who takes care of my children & the lady who caters my parties & the lady who accepts quarters at the bathroom in sardi's. those poor creatures shd be sterilized/ no one shd have to live such a life. cd you hand me a towel/ thank-you caroline. i've left all of maxime's last winter clothes in a pile for you by the back door. they have to be cleaned but i hope yr girls can make gd use of them.

    oh/ i'm still not being fair/ all the white women in the world dont wake up being glad they aint niggahs/ only some of them/ the ones who dont/ wake up thinking how can i survive another day of this culturally condoned incompetence. i know i'll play a tenor horn & tell all the colored artists i meet/ that now i'm just like them/ i'm colored i'll say cuz i have a struggle too. or i cd punish this white beleagered body of mine with the advances of a thousand ebony bodies/ all built like franco harris or peter tosh/ a thousand of them may take me & do what they want/ cuz i'm so sorry/ yes i'm so sorry they were born niggahs. but then if i cant punish myself to death for being white/ i certainly cant in good conscience keep waiting for the cleaning lady/ & everytime i attempt even the smallest venture into the world someone comes to help me/ like if i do anything/ anything at all i'm extending myself as a white girl/ cuz part of being a white girl is being absent/ like those women who are just with a man but whose names the black people never remember/ they just say oh yeah his white girl waz with him/ or a white girl got beat & killed today/ why someone will say/ cuz some niggah told her to give him her money & she said no/ cuz she thought he realized that she waz a white girl/ & he did know but he didnt care/ so he killed her & took the money/ but the cops knew she waz a white girl & cdnt be killed by a niggah especially/ when she had awready said no. the niggah was sposed to hop round the corner backwards/ you dig/ so the cops/ found the culprit within 24 hours/ cuz just like emmett till/ niggahs do not kill white girls.

    i'm still in my house/ having flung my hair-do for the last time/ what with having to take 20 valium a day/ to consider the ERA/ & all the men in the world/ & my ignorance of the world/ it is overwhelming. i'm so glad i'm colored. boy i cd wake up in the morning & think abt anything. i can remember emmett till & not haveta smile at anybody.

    maxine (compelled to speak by natalie's pain)
whenever these things happened to me/ & i waz young/ i wd eat a lot/ or buy new fancy underwear with rhinestones & lace/ or go to the movies/ maybe call a friend/ talk to made-up boyfriends til dawn. this waz when i waz under my parents' roof/ & trees that grew into my room had to be cut back once a year/ this waz when the birds sometimes flew thru the halls

of the house as if the ceilings were sky & i/ simply another winged
creature. yet no one around me noticed me especially. no one around saw
anything but a precocious brown girl with peculiar ideas. like during the
polio epidemic/ i wanted to have a celebration/ which nobody cd
understand since iron lungs & not going swimming waznt nothing to
celebrate. but i explained that i waz celebrating the bounty of the lord/
which more people didnt understand/ til i went on to say that/ it waz
obvious that god had protected the colored folks from polio/ nobody
understood that. i did/ if god had made colored people susceptible to
polio/ then we wd be on the pictures & the television with the white
children. i knew only white folks cd get that particular disease/ & i
celebrated. that's how come i always commemorated anything that
affected me or the colored people. according to my history of the colored
race/ not enough attention was paid to small victories or small personal
defeats of the colored. i celebrated the colored trolley driver/ the colored
basketball team/ the colored blues singer/ & the colored light heavy weight
champion of the world. then too/ i had a baptist child's version of high
mass for the slaves in new orleans whom i had read abt/ & i tried to grow
watermelons & rice for the dead slaves from the east. as a child i took on
the burden of easing the ghost-colored-folks' souls & trying hard to keep
up with the affairs of my own colored world.

    when i became a woman, my world got smaller. my grandma closed
up the windows/ so the birds wdnt fly in the house any more. waz bad
luck for a girl so yng & in my condition to have the shadows of flying
creatures over my head. i didnt celebrate the trolley driver anymore/ cuz
he might know i waz in this condition. i didnt celebrate the basketball
team anymore/ cuz they were yng & handsome/ & yng & handsome cd
mean trouble. but trouble waz when white kids called you names or beat
you up cuz you had no older brother/ trouble waz when someone died/ or
the tornado hit yr house/ now trouble meant something abt yng &
handsome/ & white or colored. if he waz yng & handsome that meant
trouble. seemed like every one who didnt have this condition/ so birds
cdnt fly over yr head/ waz trouble. as i understood it/ my mama & my
grandma were sending me out to be with trouble/ but not to get into
trouble. the yng & handsome cd dance with me & call for sunday supper/
the yng & handsome cd write my name on their notebooks/ cd carry my
ribbons on the field for gd luck/ the uncles cd hug me & chat for hours abt
my growing up/ so i counted all 492 times this condition wd make me
victim to this trouble/ before i wd be immune to it/ the way colored folks
were immune to polio.

    i had discovered innumerable manifestations of trouble: jealousy/
fear/ indignation & recurring fits of vulnerability that lead me right back to
the contradiction i had never understood/ even as a child/ how half the

114

world's population cd be bad news/ be yng & handsome/ & later/ eligible &
interested/ & trouble.

plus/ according to my own version of the history of the colored
people/ only white people hurt little colored girls or grown colored
women/ my mama told me only white people had social disease &
molested children/ and my grandma told me only white people committed
unnatural acts. that's how come i knew only white folks got polio/
muscular dystrophy/ sclerosis/ & mental illness/ this waz all verified by
the television. but i found out that the colored folks knew abt the same
vicious & disease-ridden passions that the white folks knew.

the pain i succumbed to each time a colored person did something
that i believed only white people did waz staggering. my entire life seems
to be worthless/ if my own folks arent better than white folks/ then surely
the sagas of slavery & the jim crow hadnt convinced anyone that we were
better than them. i commenced to buying pieces of gold/ 14 carat/ 24
carat/ 18 carat gold/ every time some black person did something that waz
beneath him as a black person & more like a white person. i bought gold
cuz it came from the earth/ & more than likely it came from south africa/
where the black people are humiliated & oppressed like in slavery. i wear
all these things at once/ to remind the black people that it cost a lot for us
to be here/ our value/ can be known instinctively/ but since so many black
people are having a hard time not being like white folks/ i wear these gold
pieces to protest their ignorance/ their disconnect from history. i buy gold
with a vengeance/ each time someone appropriates my space or my time
without permission/ each time someone is discourteous or actually cruel
to me/ if my mind is not respected/ my body toyed with/ i buy gold/ &
weep. i weep as i fix the chains round my neck/ my wrists/ my ankles. i
weep cuz all my childhood ceremonies for the ghost-slaves have been in
vain. colored people can get polio & mental illness. slavery is not
unfamiliar to me. no one on this planet knows/ what i know abt gold/ abt
anything hard to get & beautiful/ anything lasting/ wrought from pain. no
one understands that surviving the impossible is sposed to accentuate the
positive aspects of a people.

*(alec is the only member of the company able to come immediately to maxine. when
he reaches her, lou, in his full magician's regalia, freezes the whole company)*

lou

yes yes yes   3 wishes is all you get
    scarlet ribbons for yr hair
    a farm in mississippi
    someone to love you madly
all things are possible

but aint no colored magician in his right mind
gonna make you white
cuz this is blk magic you lookin at
& i'm fixin you up good/ fixin you up good & colored
& you gonna be colored all yr life
& you gonna love it/ bein colored/ all yr life
colored & love it/ love it/ bein colored

*(lou beckons the others to join him in the chant, "colored & love it." it becomes a
serious celebration, like church/ like home/ but then lou freezes them suddenly.)*

lou
crackers are born with the right to be
alive/ i'm making ours up right here
in yr face/ & we gonna be
colored & love it

*(the huge minstrel mask comes down as company continues to sing "colored & love it/
love it being colored." blackout/ but the minstrel mask remains visible. the company
is singing "colored & love it being colored" as audience exits)*

116

The Love Space Demands

A Continuing Saga

for my beaux,
C. L. R. James and Romare Bearden

Introduction

After two weeks struggling with writing an
introduction to *The Love Space Demands* and *I Heard
Eric Dolphy in His Eyes* I headed off to my Women's
Meeting with desperation. There I confessed that I
was having trouble writing about love poems I
myself had created, plus I was confusing them with
a collection of black erotica I was to review. I begged
for assistance. Watching the women in my group
suppress giggles, raise eyebrows, and wiggle in their
seats, I realized that we all were having trouble
separating love from sex, sensuality from affection,
devotion from masochism, and independence from
fear of intimacy. I hurried from the meeting to get a
very rare hamburger from an express-gourmet-deli
near a truck stop in my neighborhood. In other
words, to rid myself of the anticipatory "rush" I was
experiencing from single-minded attention to my
visions of lust and love, I took myself someplace
familiar, but rarefied, to indulge in raw pleasure. I
could not scoop up an adequate lover or boyfriend or
sex partner or companion or intimate (I am
reluctant to make a choice even about what the
person is), but in the absence of such a counterpart, I
ate alla this hamburger. I don't eat red meat much,

but then, a luscious love (romantic or sensual episode), is, also, singular.

The epiphany of orgasms or infatuations is a consistently sought after reward for leading an otherwise reasonable life. But the transmissions of sexual diseases, including AIDS, now associated with such coming together weighs heavily on choices baby-boomers had come to make with leisure. Now, sex-death is not a Victorian metaphor for chastity. Sex-death has given birth to a whole new slew of epithets and lines meant to get somebody something they wanted, regardless of the threat to the integrity of language or love. So, monogamy is tossed around like a football or a college freshman at a frat party gone mad. Women who seek to fullfill their own sexual and sensual requisites are, again, sluts and loose. Unwanted children and pregnancies blight relationships and lives, leaving women and men baffled and angry with one another.

Our behaviors were just beginning to change when the epidemic began, moving sex closer to shame now than any time since I've been alive. Words and attitudes that undermine trust and liberty to feel are creeping back into the bedrooms and couches of our lives, so that we are always second-guessing each other. When that fails, the artificial highs of cocaine, crack, methamphetamine, heroin, alcohol, compulsive sex or compulsive suffering come sauntering down the street and into our vacant, yearning lives. The sanctity of an inner quiet and clarity present in the spirit is the least that opening up to another person requires. When we don't know what we mean or why we are doing what we do, we are only able to bring chaos and pain to ourselves and others.

120

I didn't know what was being said to me, sometimes. Sometimes, I couldn't fathom why any of us were doing what we were doing and calling ourselves somebody's beloved. The poems and monologues in *The Love Space Demands* and *I Heard Eric Dolphy in His Eyes* are real questions I have asked and the sharp edges of the answers.

The Promise/ The Premise

This poem was written in response to Robert Mapplethorpe's photographs of black men/ to be used at his request as an introduction to his *Black Book*.

irrepressibly bronze, beautiful & mine

i.

all my life they've been near me
these men/
        some for a while like the
friend of my father's who drove
each summer from denver to
st. louis/ with some different
white woman/ i remember one seemed
to like me/ she had rose blond hair
i wondered/ why do you like me
you're with him & he's mine
he's colored/ he'll always be
like that/ like me/ i think
he knew my eight-year-old
precocious soul was hankering
for days to come with one/
one of them colored fellas
who'd be mine/ on purpose/ not
just cause of some pigmentation
problem/ or a grandfather clause
in mississippi/ i lived there near
the water/ the river/ the silt
caking my calves/ me laughin with
the younguns/ the boys who'd be
black men one day
                if they lived so long

he brought me rocks/ each sojourn
quartz marble granite & sandstone

onyx ovals i could hold onto when
he drove off with the white woman
i never felt sad/ i didn't know i might
be experiencing rejection/ a little
colored girl with an ebony stone
in the palm of her hand
i knew that was his heart
where could a man go without his heart
a child by the mississippi grasping
dreams/ yet to grab holto a man
but nighttime & motown asked me to dance
sang sweet streams of sweat
moist kisses/ those arrogant torsos
daring crackers or a fool to
look the wrong way/ no just look
a funny way & it'd be over
or just begun

look at me pretty niggah

bring it over here/ i'm grown
now & the stones don't sit
static in my hand/ you know
how it is black volcanoes erupt
they say when miles davis manages
to whisper/ they erupt they say
when the blackstone rangers take
a stroll/ black volcanoes seep
lava anywhere there's true love
now i'm not talkin about
a hoot and holler or a dance on a dime
but whenever there's true
love/ black volcanoes seep lava
& it's always been mine

always my dear like the Bible
says an eye for an eye/ there's
a me for a you

       bring it on baby
i've been holding your heart in
my hand since i was a child
i've been preoccupied on occasion
       but i had to grow some too
cause i wanted what all you were
what all you are/ now you're a man
you've got the world watchin your
every move/ i've got your heart
& by the mississippi/ when i was a
    child/ we callt that a groove
sweet black-eyed pea
honey dripped husk

    bring it on/ i'm not afraid

i've known you all my life
       & this my dear is just the
beginning
the first inkling of what they're gonna
          hear
it ain't no lie that we could sing
don't be embarrassed/ just appear
right there
       the way i have you/ those
times you're brown & wet/ those
times your strength can't be met
just be
       &
remember me/ oh back then

when you rode off & left
      your heart in the palm
      of my child hand

II.

he's of course george jackson
doing push-ups and visiting with angela

soledad   soledad

confined to his beauty alone
fighting cement walls for air
malcolm's last breath king's crumbling torso
speak to me of beauty
blood beauty courage sweating rage
of course he's lumumba
see only the eyes/ bob marley wail
in the night ralph featherstone
burning temples as pages of books
become ashen and smolder by his ankles
walter rodney's blood fresh soakin
the streets/ leon damas spoke poems
with this face/ césaire cursed our
enemies/ making welcome our true voice
the visage of a people
continually mourning
recognized our beauty so slowly
our heroes fade like jackie wilson
in silence/ in the still of the night

soledad mi amor soledad

III.

among palms whistling lizards
nestle by roots freshly humid
roots by palm fronds the sun
tickles lovers inviting them to
make quickly some love in
moist sands seeping through toes
pull down the bosom the legs
wiry & thick haired pull down
the petticoats/ lace panties
perfumed lips skipping over
shoulders muscles making music
where before only acacias & macaws
dared solo/ many duets
have been abandoned by the trunks
of palms searching for
moonlight/ rushing toward the sky
as tongues would wrap round
each other/ dew like honey
slipping from their lips
whole skies fallen by
their feet/

jaguars prowl when their
eyes meet.

The Love Space Demands

even tho yr sampler broke down on you

magnolias & forsythia blossom
from yr Sugar Hill/ Ray Drummond
plays nasty riffs & i imagine
alla the Palm Cafe turns out
when you glow at dusk on
Convent Avenue/ slidin easily by
the just-for-us propositions Gylan Kain
fashioned at every other Harlem corner/
we usedta leave deluxe issues of
love potions/ remedies even insinuations
danglin from Baptist steeples/ Methodist steps
jump back/ jump up/ beatin down/ flyin
yng wenches whose skirts still
tease solos over to the Savoy/

    (you cd make yrself irresistible/ be my
       Willis Avenue Bridge/ floatin/ Rican wet
         su lengua dulce/ over an East River of
           gardenias/ remember the minor sixth)
you hummed to me while I was
reachin for the/ ceilin/ where our
folks was carryin on before Michelangelo
or Lionel Richie/ some where round there
where you brush up gainst baobabs/ well
        (you know where my beauty marks are/ all
over
HARLEM)
we sing like flowers/ i see
round brown honies giggle at us/ the
silly/ niggahness of yr quick light

kisses/ *cómo* fresh/ *mi chabalo negro/ mi propio* Tito
Puente/
    my own rhythmn section/ that petal
  openin evey time yr lips/ let
love/ *cada vez/* yr lips
let love fall/ all
over
Sugar Hill

serial monogamy

i think/ we should reexamine/ serial monogamy
is it/ one at a time or
one for a long time?
                    how
does the concept of infinity relate to a skilled
serial monogamist/ & can
that person consider a diversionary escapade
a serial
one night stand?
                    can a consistent
serial monogamist
have one/ several/ or myriad relationships
that broach every pore of one's body
    so long as there is no penetration?
do we/ consider adventurous relentless tongues
capable of penetration & if we do
can said tongues whip thru us indiscriminately
with words/ like

                    "hello"
    "oh, you lookin good"
    "you jigglin, baby"
cd these be reckless immature violations of
serial monogamy?

    i mean/
if my eyes light up cuz
    some stranger just lets go/ caint stop hisself
from sayin
            "yr name must be paradise"
    if i was to grin or tingle/ even get a lil happy/

135

        hearin me & paradise/ now synonyms
does that make me a scarlet woman?
        if i wear a red dress that makes someone else hot
        does that put me out the fryin pan & into the
fire?

say/
my jade bracelet got hot
                (which aint possible cuz jade aint
jade
                if it aint cold)
but say
my jade got lit up & burst offa my wrist
& i say/
        "i gotta find my precious stones
cuz they my luck"
                & he say
"luck don't leave it goes where
you need it"
                & i say
"i gotta find my bracelet"
                & he say
"you know for actual truth
                you was wearin this bracelet?"
& i say
  "a course, it's my luck"
                & he say
"how you know?"
& i say
        "cuz
        i heard my jade
        flyin thru the air
        over yr head

                behind my knees
                &
                up under the Japanese lampshade!"
                    & he say
    "you heard yr jade flyin thru the air?"
                "yes"
                    i say
    "& where were they flyin from"
                he say
            "from my arm" i say
            "they got hot & jumped offa my arm"
    "but/
    where was yr arm?"
                he say
    & i caint say mucha nothin
    cuz
    where my arm was a part a some tremendous
    current/
    cd be 'lectricity or niggahs on fire/
    so where my arm was is where/ jade gets hot
    & does that imply the failure of serial monogamy?

    do flamin flyin jade stones
    on a arm/ that is a kiss/ & a man who knows where/
    luck is
    take the serial/ outta monogamy/ & leave
    love?

intermittent celibacy

listenin to bobby timmons & jackie wilson
does not encourage abstinence/
& it's not like smokey misled me/ either/
i cdn't get nobody to let me be a bad girl &
how i tried to get one of them/ to make me
a woman/
let me out the deprivations of virginty
                        anna mae wong's fans
                        flutterin
                        over audrey hepburn's shorn
                        head
                        in fronta the cross/
                        Holy Mary Mother of God/
let somebody else come take me/
                        surely
                        The Lord God Almighty
gotta 'nough virgins
to make a rich mullah
forsake Muhammed/
                        (figuratively speaking of
                        course)
all i wanted
was to be/ revealed
& that's what happens to alla us
like/ unto
                        Mary   Isis   Oshun
                        Kali   Ishtar   Tlalozlatl
to leave the sexual covenant
of the   Father
    some other man/ has to make you bleed,
but

it gets better/
there are other fingers tongues loins hair/
everywhere
sweat/ sounds no one's ever heard/ an achin quiet
makes yearnin for salvation/ minor penance
all

this you can/ suffer
all
this/ minglin breath & cum
like the nectar offered on Olympus
from yr tongue to his cheek/ & his
shoulder/ the river niger is flowin/ &
you've fallen/ from

                        Grace

my dear/
you gave it up/ & now
whatchu gonna keep?

                        memories of inchoate
                        union
                the mole on his left leg
            chantin at the ashram
        you say you gave up meat
you thought you were a
    gift of god/
                        you close yr legs to the flesh
but does that fill you/ with the Holy Ghost?
is/ not runnin off with that pretty
muthafuckah you been hankerin after/
a spirit-filled occasion?
                        if/
you don't allow nobody
to touch you in the bed you share
                        but

the southeastern coast of france
is some/ other/ where you
available?

                    can

you touch yrself

                    &

when you do/ do you rush to say
"get thee behind me
Satan?"

                 or

has/ the devil caressed yr eyebrows
left you/ gaspin
for/ just one mo
temptation?

                         is it/ okay/
                         to wait a week
                         or/ say
                         change the sheets?

you know/
it's been a day & a half
      since i had any/
& do any you've had
know you/ that you
a gift of god
& the devil's mistress/

                         abstinence
                         is not
                         celibacy

cuz/ when you filled with the Holy Ghost
every man/ in the world
can smell it/

                         you wake up drippin
                         with the
                         spirit

doves perch by yr clit
cooin with the drifters
til the paragons & the jesters
come/ flyin all they colors
lay claim/ to yr moans
bring you right up to em
with/ the "wind"
oh-oh-oh wind   wind

chastening with honey

by all rites i shd be writin
right to left/ upside down
or backwards/
speech/ shd run garbled & dyslexic thru my
brain/ til i hear yr voice
clearly/ again/

in some other/ life were you a mandala?
are you "OM"?
is shakti-pat/ yr regular metabolic status/
under ordinary circumstances?
oh/ there I go again
admirin myself/ unwittingly/
invitin some terribly/ lush *mot palabra son syllable*/
to flail
abt my bangs & lashes
so moist/ you smile/ i remember/ this is arrogance
& it's over

this/ chastening with honey
is nothin/ like the Passion of Christ/
which brought us Lent & we give up meat/
quit our lust/ for blood & bonbons/
Mohammed's trials brought Ramadan/ & we may only
quench our thirst for life from dawn to dusk/
& Buddha/ neath the bo tree/ spread joy abt our
ankles
so long as we rid ourselves of resentment &
impatience/ now Krishna/ is another kind of story/
but goatherds & goatherdesses/ sheperds &
sheperdesses/
all come with chastening.

142

you may/ sheer this wool/ wet it
braid it til you can wrap it round/ two or three
parallel/ cosmic strings/
just don't/ disrupt the ritual
the leap from maya to nirvana/ overwhelms
unwitting/ arrogance
& *je ne sais que ton insouciance*/ we
can't handle passion/ with the deftness
we associate with civil servants/ in Ibadan or
Bogota/
i am so lucky
this is the essence of life/ you
present yrself/ with the warmth of the Goddess/
the ferocity of Yahweh/ the glee of Shiva/ the
cunning of Coyote/ the de-groovi-licious breath of
Obatala/ like
there was some difference tween yr voice/ this
honey/ fallin off
my body/ & wild hummingbirds from the rain forest
appear
by the A train/ imaginin you some/ tropical flower
pollen
hoverin over Manhattan/ like the Muslim brother's
incense/
maybe/ if i burn you up/ i'd calm down/
the endorphin crazed
birds/ cd go back to the Amazon/   think abt it/
fire/ is a great rite of passage/   the pollen &
the honey & the
flyin birds by my cheek/ oh oh/ i understand/
this is the fall from the Garden.

a third generation geechee myth for yr birthday

(for John Purcell)

when we fall from the stars to the bellies of
our mothers/ some folks say
    they's music in the air/ dontcha think/
we tumble thru a niggah
night/ etchin light
        thru them black holes
unimaginable density
inconceivable radiance/ black
pitch/ maybe the air
in a black hole/ is the sacred hush of rushes round
lil baby moses/ or might cd be the fire
brightenin black holes/ is reliable
as maceo's wail/ when we glide
from planet to planet/ swing right past our own
down/ to our mothers' bellies
some folks say
    they's a storm a comin/
& the sea belts the shores/ how
ben webster burst thru a eye of a hurricane/
gilmore singin volcanic steam/ fool enough
to rise up from ashes/ molten glowin
      any kinda dead fire
caint/ fly out no niggah night/
    to our mothers' bellies/ caint lead us
outta black hole/ slyly shepp or
prophet ayler/ overwhelming pressure
epistemologically/ impossible constructs/
left bird & dapper lester/ outside kansas city
goin somewhere/ must be/ on our way

144

cuz/ we done come careenin out severely colored
stratospheres/
surgin with the force of them/ what
am in the tradition/ & them what aint
caint/ smoke cigars or make light in a white hole
either/
be like playin a tenor wit a trumpet
mouthpiece/ mistakin junior walker
for philip glass/ no no no/ that aint our way
when/ we come sailin out the vistas of galaxies
tip/ our hats to marshall allen/
jimmy lyons/ maybe mr. coltrane gone whiz by/
maybe not/ cd be an itinerant errant one-man-negro-
band
over to Grand Central/ but
          we all/ come gallopin out the heavens
to our mothers' bellies/ & the niggah
blue night/ you was wendin yo way
down heah/ *stars fell over alabama/ mood indigo
new grass/ ornithology/ ascension/ freedom now/
crosstown traffic*
& *"i wonder who's lovin you"/ "better stop doggin me
around"*
"blase"/ say hey/ *"friends & neighbors"/ "doncha
know you make me wanna
shout"* flew/ out yr mother's mouth
          you/ burst out her body
          & that's how/ you come to be
          a reed man/

loosening strings or give me an 'A'

yes/ i listened to country joe & the fish/
    yes/ i howled with steppenwolf/
yes/ fleetwood mac was my epiphany/
   & creedance clearwater revival
swept me neath the waters/   hendrix
my national anthem always/ yes
  blind lemon jefferson & b. b. huddle
by my stage door/ yes chuck berry lives
next to me/ yes
     eric clapton made me wanna have
         a child named layla/   yes
sonny sharrock drew screams outta me
         linda can't eclipse/
yes/ i remember My Lai & the Audubon debacle
yes/ hamza-el-din is a caracole out my mouth
yes/ i never forgot where i came from &
nobody misses me cuz/
            i never left
  in search of a portrait
      of an artist
        as a yng man/
yes   i read ULYSSES & he came home
         yes/ oh/ yes
             i know my/ Joyce
i cd tell niggah chords meant for me/
yes/ "I searchin . . . I'm searchin"/ my Olympics say
Circe/ the Scylla the Charybdis/
          any Siren & all the Pentagon
yes/ Circe/ the Scylla/ the Charybdis,
    any Siren/ and alla the Pentagon/
aint kept/ yes/ i say/ aint kept

this one/ yes/ niggah man/ from/ yes
                    makin art outta me/
yes/
      "i'm gonna love him all over/ all over/
              & over & over"
cuz niggahs aint in search of/
      we/ just get discovered
so/ yes
   i must be the New World now/ yes
i'm in tune
oh/ yes/ play me
                  . pick/ my colored tones
   yes/ strum my niggah/ chords
                  find/ my sharps & flats
let em/ have/ space
oh/ yes oh/ yes/ i know my Joyce
& Ulysses/ he done come home
yes/ play me/ now
yes/ make me alla that
yes/ i'll be the bottom or i cd just ride
yes/ i know my Joyce/ & all you gotta say/ is
      "Give me a 'A'"
      Ahhhhhhhhhhhhhhhhh
yes/ Ulysses he done come home
yes/ i must be the New World
yes/ Ulysses he done come home
yes/ i must be the New World
yes/ i'm in tune
just/ yes/ oh yes/ just play me
   baby/ play me/
                  yes/

mesl (male english as a second language): in defense of bilingualism

i watch black & white movies the way
    yall hanker after the World Series
not like i'm on first base or nothin
    & i surely won't be pitchin
but i do know how to walk em or
              bring in three wit one hit to the far
outfield

yeah.

i hadda brother & he showed me some things.

but
i learnt what i know bout game-playin
    on saturdays fore dawn on reruns
        of who for you are Jim Brown & Willie Mays/
    when i fly i don't condense to a pigskin
ellipse or a leather suited billiard ball
    popped outta Yankee Stadium
who for you is ecstasy on Wrigley Field
    is Tyrone Power as Zorro
        Ronald Coleman seekin out the
        Guillotine for my honor
not my chastity or my reputation/
        Ronald Coleman's deliberately
    riskin himself cuz/ he loved me so
just on accounta he had offered himself
              to me/
he'd die
    fore that gift was took from me.

there are no umpires/ in my game
  & no men in lil striped shirts/ usin
    sign language
      deaf women don't understand/

hey/

we go for broke/ where i suit up/ but
    i caint say 'xactly where that is
less/ i buy me 19 acres & some astroturf/
    yall got no clarity/ bout what game
      it is we playin.

so/
i'ma talk to you the best i can/
awright/

here's the whole/ 9/ yards/
    i'm the black queen/ but
  that don't make this chess/ cuz
kings don't hold no sway here/ like pawns
  they come & go/
                this aint football/ cuz men
                whose faces i caint see/ don't get
close enough to me/ to tackle nothin/
      & i'm not the quarterback/ cuz
    low-riders don't waste alla they
  hydraulic wizardry/ on nothin
that aint a whole lotta somethin/
    i cd be a goalie/ but why i'm
gone stand round myself wit a crooked stick?
& i have no desire/ to bounce balls
  offa my head/ in fronta
    thousands of people

when i swim
   i'm not aimin for the other side/
   i'm warm waters/ inchin thru coral
lookin to galavant/ on a dolphin's back.

what's the rush abt?

            you caint make a dolphin into a gazelle
         in less than 30,000 years/
      if i take my time
   i might come upon Shangri-la/ Mt. Fuji
                           long fore yall gotta
                           national holiday for
Satchel Paige
                     or convince the five
percenters
                        they aint the only ones goin
to Heaven/
                     while they mock Malcom & call
alla
            the rest of us/ they "earths"

whatchu think you standin on?

Diamonds?
Diamonds/ deep in South Africa/ or Chicago?
      you think you are really
            on the Stairway
               to Heaven?
that/ you the decidin factor/ in
            overtime/ hey

did you ever go to the movies/
        & know
    you/ the hero?

(i caint be no Scarlet/ if you caint find Charleston/ &
the Blue Dahlia/ aint nothin but another bar/ less
you give me
them flowers/ & Sally caint meet Harry/ or Tom or
Dick/
til you ready/ for a feature film)
this/ is really the bottom line.

        i love/ black & white movies/
that's/ the world i was born to/ alla
        them pastel circles round/ neptune/
        rose quartz moon's flirtin wit saturn/
    rouge hues over mars/
    are outer space to me/

& i do/ wanna play wit you/

    i don't wanta win/ necessarily/
        that'd be nice/ but it's how you
say/ "engagée"/ that stirs me & scares you/

in my ballpark/ nobody's decimated/ nobody's
        a loser/   but
it can get rough/

(we cd leave the Astrodome/ in alla our regalia/ &
nobody'd
know/
no/ where
no/ way

151

who'd won or lost
what)
but/
   they'd know somethin happened/
there was some back breakin/ knee twistin/
shoulder dislocatin/ leapin gainst the
leftfield fence/ shin-splintin/ bitin dust/
umpire cursin/ slidin into home
fandangle/

     oh/
     they'd know/

that's/ how i play
          that's how i play/ everything/

but/ you say/
   "everything seems to work out
          when we talk it over in bed"

hum/

if you cd slam-dunk it/ maybe i'd
          rush the goalposts carryin blue satin/
          string the basket wit red silk/
          ·oil yr body wit mine/

HEY/ HEY/ WHAT D'YA SAY/
          wit some discipline/ 9-3-36-41/
GOOD GOD?
          you might even match my stayin power!
OOOOOOOH . . . let's see/ that/ again/ slowly/
          frame by frame/ imagine that backhand/ pass/
why isaiah thomas/ cdn't have asked for a more/

perfect/ YES
this is America's genius . . .
can you/
did you ever see that move?
have/
you ever seen that/ kind of co-or-di- . . .
did you catch that?
cd you see?

OOOOOOOOHHHHHHHHHHHHHHHHHH!
whatta game/

hey/

do you wanna play wit me?

devotion to one lover or another

i bathe in gardenia scented
water/ amaryllis fricia & white tulips
move-to-&-from me the way brazen niggahs
what cd dance do when it suit them/ flower
petals lavender coral ivory *rojo amarillo pretu/*
yes/ black petals/ float & open like i do when
i am a devoted lover/ my baths are rituals
like cock crows & cornbread/ but aint a
lover i been devoted to ever known/ thought
abt/ bothered/ or imagined what kinda flowers
should creep over my breasts/ the bubbles & steam
cleanse me of all extraneous energies/ dirt
the earth forces her ravenous scent outta
me/ less i halfway fricassee my definitively
sensate geechee body/ hot hot waters gotta
seduce my muscles/ stretch me/ exorcize
them toxins/ the flower petals
carry danger way from me
this method of survival
has yet to be detected/

it's a pity no one has ever thought
to put you in a tub of flowers
where yr loveliness/ niggah/
is unencumbered/
just steamin
now/ how to stay clean/
we all know white folks
carry lice/ but the world is fulla vermin
what'll kill a something fragile as a love/ & yes
we had good times/ they was beauty there/

so startlin/ as to obscure the veritable north star
but i am not awash in lovers/ quite like that/
it's the ones i cursed/ threw bottles at/ &
plain made myself a ravin fool over/ they
understand my survival/ that i'm still here/
that/ whatever inarticulate desires
we rocked & rolled jus haveta stop demandin
so much/ but that yen to touch/ that
upper lip ever so/ feel yr head up under
them arms/ that/
don't go away/ it stops askin are you awready?
even if i/ kicked him down the stairs/
threw all the damn horns out the window/
that there yen for that touch/ don't care/
& it's time to take a bath/
bedrock don't grow orchids/
i wanna be washed in white tulips/
scarlet amaryllis/ & gardenias/
muthahfuckahs jus caint/ get this together/
i even know some body who wdn't run my water/
& it don't matter to me none/ if
you do think i'm out my rightful mind/
        i say/ lovin is more than pleasurin/
which cd run off with any sense you got/
cause/ devotion is sustenance/
& i know what cleans me/ feeds me/
flowers
earth's offered up/ so beautifully
they can float off from me/ with
all this dirt/
we colored & in love/
we in mortal danger/
i don't bathe in wild flowers/ for nothin/

**"If I go all the way without you
where would I go?"**

—The Iseley Brothers

there/ to the right of venus
                    close to where yr lion
stalks our horizon/   see/
listen/
glow scarlet/ char-scarlet/ set my heart down
there/   near you/ scaldin *amarillo/*
oh/ say/ my new day
                    . my dawn/
yr fingers trace the rush of my lips/
                         ever so reverent/
                              ever so hungry/

here/
to the right side of venus/
                         my tongue/
                    tropical lightenin/
rush/ now/ softly/ tween my toes/ the seas ebb
& in these sands/ i've come back/
                    an unpredictible swell
a fresh water lily/ in the north atlantic/
when you touch me/   yes
that's how pearls somehow/ rip from the white of my
bones
   to yr fingertips/
     incontrovertible hard chicago/
                    rococo implications/
& this/   the mississippi delta/ tween my thighs
yr second touch/ forbids
a thing less/ than primordial fluidity/

156

no/
i lay next to you/
       the undertow at carmel/
the russian river/ feelin up stalks of the best/ of
humboldt county
& damn it/
         what makes you think/ my spine is
yr personal/
san andreas fault?

            shiftin/ serene fields break for rain/
til
i open/ deep brown moist & black
        cobalt sparklin everywhere/
we are
there/
       where the pacific fondles my furthest
shores/ detroit-high-russet/ near redwoods/
      i am climbin
          you chase me/ from limb to limb/
             pullin/ the colored stars/ out the
night
              slippin em/ over my tongue/
&
i thought i cd get over/
the dangers/ of livin
      on the pacific rim/
when i look at you/
i
know/ i am riskin my life/
   tossin reason/ to the outback of the far
rockaways/
         goin/ givin up/ everything/ with out
protest/

givin up/ meteorological episodes
the appalachian mountains/
                          handin over/ islands from puget
sound/
                    travis county hill country/
givin away/ treasures/
i
never
claimed/
      til i felt you/

my own december sunset/ teasin cypress/
even campbell street bikers/ in downtown oakland/
i stopped resistin/
what won't/ be orderly/ imagined/ legitimate/
yes/ yes/
hold me
like/ the night grabs wyoming/
& i am more/ than i am not/
i cd sing sacred lyrics/ to songs i don't know/
my cheek/ rubs gainst the nappy black/ cacti of yr
chest/
& i am a flood/ of supernovas/
if you kiss me like that/ i'm browned wetlands
yr lips/ invite the moon/ to meander/
our mouths open & sing/
yes/
our tongues/
the edge of the earth/

I Heard Eric Dolphy in His Eyes

"I Heard Eric Dolphy in His Eyes," is a performance piece designed to explore the violence and lyricism, the incongruities and the constants, as well as the magic and limitations of Afro-American urban life and our music that documents our realities and sometimes impossible yearnings for peaceful, nurturing actualities.

The company of six (three musicians, three dancer/actresses) explicates the exigencies of reality versus possibility through five monologues and four dance sequences; all involve interaction with the musicians as well as fragments of Dolphy compositions and solos. The rhythms and language of the monologues compells the movement and music that lead us to the next spoken words. Some things fall easily into speech, while others defy verbal exegesis, available only through music, and the fluid or percussive eloquence of the human body in motion.

i heard eric dolphy in his eyes

yesterday evenin/ no/ mo like last night/ the
moon took on a scarlet hue/ *lune rouge/ luna
roja/ una luna loca/ soy yo una loquita/*
thru mists & the clouds that mix
wit neon invitations & tears unshed/ tears
waitin for tomorrow/ i met the 7th Avenue IRT
Express/ specially tailored for Malcolm X Boulevard
& the computerized palettes at the
Schomberg/ the train came whistling by/ deluxe
from 145th Street/ to my heart/ throbbin
& seekin rhythms not uncomfortable wit wind
chill factors & smog what cd mix wit neon &
cloud/ hoverin/ by the base of hydrants
ferocious brazen legs of young girls seein to
their own undoin/
    "Rah, Rah"
i says/ is this a football game
    "Rah, Rah"

i says/ the Knicks must be playin at
155th Street/ in the chill spill of the night/
    "Rah, Rah"
the march/ is movin on to Howard Beach/
another day/ of outrage/
    "Rah, Rah"
must be Daniel Ortega/ or Fidel/ back
on a terrace/ wit confetti & chicken
feathers/ cheers of absolution/
cheers/ proclaimin the comin/ of
a new day/
    "Rah, Rah"

come a voice/ pummelin/ like a
bulldozer/ come a voice too usedta pain/
        "Rah, Rah"
the child's tumblin/ from one pole to
the next/ his filthy tattered snowsuit
mo accustomed/ to bein spat on/
than makin angels/ the cold nibbles his
naked lil feet/ he cries/ this baby who can
barely walk/ cuz he simply
is too young/ now/ the child cries & smiles
at the same time/ deaf to his own name/
        "Rah, Rah"
                "niggah/ get up off da floor/ ya heah
me?

                git yo black ass off da floor/ niggah/ ya
heah me?"
the child/ RahRah/ shoulda been
praised/ he tries so hard/ he tries
he tries/ so hard/ he reaches/ wit his lil
arms for the hard grey plastic of the
subway bench/ he pulls his pink-smudged feet
up/ offa the ground/ but/ not fast enough
cuz the voice/ that barrelin
crude/ nasty ol voice/ keeps chasin the
child/ up & up & up/ to the seat/ &
then/ the po child falls back down/ on
top the comic strips from the *Daily News*/ the
Times OpEd page/ the personals from *The Advocate*/
& miscellaneous/ spiritual opportunities featured in
the *Amsterdam News*/ proclaimin that only
one/ Papa Legbé visited Harlem each
year/ & only one/ love could save us from
misfortune/ & only one/ child was
hoisted by the seat of his pants/ nose

first down on the hard littered
bench/ where the hand of the voice
the fist of the low-down muthafuckah
crashed into the flesh & marrow of a child
who can barely talk/ or walk/ who has mastered
the art of weepin & smilin/ at the
same time/ a child who raises his arms like
like he gonna hug the voice/
    "Rah, Rah"
he's lookin/ at all of us/
the fists/ ricochet off his
temple to his calves/ smilin &
cryin/ wishin/ maybe wishin/ this heah
time/ the voice won't take his dirty red
hat/ offa his scabby nappy head/ wishin
the hands of the voice/ wouldn't roll his
pants legs up/ so wazn't no way to fend off
the cold/ hopin a tambourine/ wouldn't be
set on top his stroller/ by the voice/
takin off his own shoes to balance/ on
a wooden leg/ he leans on it
when he's not beatin/
    "RahRah"

                "we gonna make some money
                tonight/ we gonna git fired up/
                awright/ yeah/ yeah tonight/
                tonight/
                gone git me/ all fired up/
                tonight"
& whack/ cross the baby's head wit
knuckles/ leavin a puffed up
bleedin space/ neath the right eye/
& the baby tries to smile/

"ladies & gentlemen/ we heah is
homeless & we'd like ya to give
us/ whatever the lord moves ya
to do/ ya know how kids are/
sometimes/ ya gotta be a lil
hard on em"
speak to me/ RahRah/ speak to me/
RahRah/ i wanna sing to ya til
there's/ no mo fog round lake michigan/
til there's/ no mo steely cacophony
just above yo head/ let ya
breathe somethin tender/ like dew/ fresh
air & someone tenderly round bout
ya/ everywhere/ i swear i heard A.I.R.
delicately triumph/ in his eyes/
tender in his eyes/ fierce/ in his eyes
i say/ i heard an A.I.R. song

i heard A.I.R. in his eyes/
RahRah/ RahRah/
i heard please/ in his sighs
i heard/ what'd i ever do to you/ in his eyes
RahRah/ RahRah/
Get up/ run for yo life/

there in his eyes in the harsh
night/ trail of whimpers & mean giggles
led a solo bassoon/ a
bass clarinet/ some sound broader mo
powerful/ than this child/ i know/ i heard
Chicago howlin thru his eyes/ when
love surfaces like crumbs/ he's
gone set up & grin/ i knew ya were heah
all along/ ya were heah/ like

164

me/ unfinished & frail/ like an A.I.R.
song/ rockin/ sadness/

i wanna know/ what love sounds like/
i wanna know/ what love sounds like
A.I.R./ fresh air/ new A.I.R./ in his eyes/
Rah Rah/ Rah Rah/
i hear don't hit me again awright
in his eyes/ cold or night/ in his eyes/
RahRah/ RahRah/
i heard/ eric dolphy in his eyes/
                    "ladies and gentlemen/ we heah is
                    homeless & we'd like ya to give
                    us/ whatever the lord moves ya
                    to do/ ya know how kids are/
                    sometimes/ ya gotta be a lil
                    hard on em"

crack annie

i caint say how it come to me/ shit
somehow/ it just come over me/ & i
heard the lord sayin how beautiful/ &
pure waz this child of mine/ & when i
looked at her i knew the Lord waz
right/ & she waz innocent/ ya know/
free of sin/ & that's how come i
gave her up to cadillac lee/ well/ how
else can i explain it/

who do ya love i wanna know i wanna know
who do ya love i wanna know i wanna know

what mo could i say

who do ya love i wanna know i wanna know
who do ya love i wanna know i wanna know

it's not like she had hair round her
pussy or nothin/ she ain't old enough
anyway for that/ & we sho know/ she
aint on the rag or nothin/ but a real
good friend of mine from round 28th
street/ he tol me point-blank
wazn't nothin in the whole world smell
like virgin pussy/ & wazn't nothin in the
universe/ taste like new pussy/ now this
is my friend talkin/ & ya know how
hard it is to keep a good man fo yo self
these days/ even though i know i got
somethin sweet & hot to offer/ even

then/ i wanted to give my man cadillac
lee/ somethin i jus don't have no mo/
new pussy/ i mean it aint dried up or
nothin/ & i still know what muscles i
cd get to work in my pussy/ this-a-way
& that but what i really wanted/ my
man/ cadillac to have for his self/ waz some
new pussy/ & berneatha waz so
pretty & sweet smellin/ even after
she be out there runnin wit the boys/
my berneatha *vida*/ waz sweet & fine
remember that song "so fine"

 so fine my baby's so doggone fine
 sends them thrills up & down my spine
 whoah-oh-oh-yeah-yeaeaeah-so-fine

well/ that's my child/ *fine*/ & well
cadillac always come thru for me/ ya
know wit my crack/ oh honey/ lemme tell
ya how close to jesus i get thanks
to my cadillac/ lemme say now/ witout
that man i'd been gone on to
worms & my grave/ but see i had me
some new pussy/ waz my daughter/ lemme
take that back/ i didn't have none/
any new pussy/ so i took me some/ & it
jus happened to be berneatha/ my
daughter/ & he swore he'd give me twenty-five
dollars & a whole fifty cent of crack/
whenever/ i wanted/ but you know/ i'm on the pipe/
& i don't have no new pussy/ & what difference/
could it
make/ i mean shit/ she caint get pregnant/
shit/ she only seven years old

& these scratches/ heah/ by my fingers
that's/ where my child held onto
me/ when the bastard/ cadillac/ took
her like she wazn't even new pussy at
all/ she kept lookin at me &
screamin/ "mommy/ mommy help me/ help
me"/ & all i did waz hold her
tighter/ like if i could stop her
blood from circulation/ if i could stop
her from hurtin/ but no/ that aint how
it went down at all/ nothin like that/
trust me/ i got scars where my
daughter's fingernails broke my skin
& then/ when he waz finished wit my
child/ cadillac/ he jump up & tell me
to cover my child's pussy/ wit some
cocaine/ so she wdn't feel nothin no
mo/ i say/ why ya aint done
that befo/ why ya wait til ya done/
to protect her/ he say/ befo i lay
you down & give ya some of the same/
dontcha know/ ya haveta hear
em scream befo ya give em any
candy/ & my lil girl heard all
this/ my child bled alla this/ & all i
could do waz to look for some more crack
wit the fifty cadillac done give
me/ but/ i wazn't lookin for it for
me/ jesus knows/ i wanted it for
berneatha/ so she wouldn't haveta
remember/ she wouldn't have to
remember/ nothin at all/ but i saw dark purple
colored marks
by her shoulder/ where i held her down for

cadillac/ i'm her mother & i held her
& if ya kill me/ i'll always know/
i'm gonna roam round hell talkin
bout new pussy/ & see my child's
blood caked bout her thighs/ my child's
shoulders purple wit her mother's
love/ jesus save me/ come get me
jesus/ now/ lord take my soul & do
wit it what ya will/ lord have
mercy/ i thought berneatha waz like
me/ that she could take anythin/ ya
know/ caint nothin kill the will of the
colored folks/ but lord i waz
wrong/ them marks on my child/ no/
not the marks/ from cadillac/ the scars
from my fingers/ purple & blue
blotches/ midnight all ruby on lenox
avenue at 7:30 on sundays/ that heavy
quiet/ that cruelty/ i caint take
no mo/ so lord throw me into hell befo
berneatha is so growed/ she do it
herself/ all by herself/ laughin
& shovin me/ & prowlin &
teasin/ sayin/ you a mother/ what
kinda mother are you/ bitch/ tell me/
now/ mommy what kinda mother/ are you/ mommy/
mommy/

i say/ i heard etta james in her eyes/ i
know/ i heard the blues in her eyes/ an
unknown/ virulent blues/ a stalkin

takin no answer but yes to me
blues/ a song of a etta james/ a
cantankerous blues/ a blues born of
wantin & longin/ wantin & longin for
you/ mama/ or etta mae/
song of a ol hand me down blues
hangin by its breath/ alone
a fragile new blues
hardly close to nowhere/ cept them eyes
& i say/ i heard a heap of etta james
in them eyes/ all over them eyes/
so come on Annie

so tell mama all about it

tell mama all about it
all about it
all about it

tell mama

running backwards/ conroe to canarsie

i.

before i was born
they said/ the Scottsboro Boys did it/
when/ i was a child/
they said/ Emmett Till did it/
now/ i'ma woman/
and my child's a child/
and they say/ Clarence Brandley did it/

some/ one of them/
some black boy/ or man/
who didn't bow his head/ or grin with teeth/
or jus was in the vicinity of/ or
with access to/ or imagined/ access
to the now/ dead white girl/
glorified/ in her decay/
sanctified/ in her
demise/
closer to God in death/ than in life/

a niggah did it/
had to be/
the Lord smite evil out the hands
of white folks/
that's how come/ they know/
a niggah did it/
ask any/ white man/ in Conroe/

Run niggah Run!   Got me a niggah this
I got ya this time!   time.
  Hey, Niggah!   Can ya hear me, boy!
  That's right, niggah   Over here!
                                    Right here!
     I been waitin for this a long time.

ii.

we's eatin pizza at the pizza shop/
when we see's these niggahs/ at the
counter talkin like they's gonna eat
some pizza too/ this/ is our
neighborhood!/ we don't have no trash in
the streets/ and niggers in the pizza
parlor at nighttime/ there's decent folks
around here & white women & my
children/ how we gonna let some niggers/
just walk in & walk out of where we
live/ like they hadda right to go
wherever they wanted to go/ so/ we
jammed em up/ ya know/ with some sticks
& tire irons & baseball bats
& our fists/ we chased em/ like runnin dogs/
cause a nigger's got to know/ not to come
around Howard Beach/ Bernard Goetz was
right/ he's my hero/ ya know/ get em
before they get you/ cause once ya let
one in/ you can't stop it/ they're like
roaches/ they come out at night.

III.

Hey Niggah!
That's right, niggah.
I been waitin for this a long time.
Run, niggah, run!
I got ya this time!

Over here!
Right here!
Got me a
        niggah this
time.
Can ya hear
        me, boy?

iv.

> *hush now/ don't explain*
> *there's nothin to gain*
> *i'm glad you're back*
> *don't explain*

did you have a black boy for his neck to
be broke/ for his father to see forsook
tell me/ cuz i wanna know/

> *hush now/ don't explain*
> *you're my joy & pain*
> *my life/ your love*
> *don't explain*

now/ somebody needs to tell me why/ my
boy's gotta die/ deep in some river/
we 'magine flowin to heaven/ oh oh . . . *hush*
now/ yo child aint to
blame/ less he gotta sign

writ all up & down his berry black back
say what/ say/ cicatrix are improvised
these days/ Lord/ Lord come by heah/ ·
this/ is the word of God/ & we a God's
children/ this heah/ is the new Jerusalem/
& apartheid is a mortal sin/ teach me/ Jesus/
tell somebody to say that/ in Crown Heights/
find me a witness/ to croon roundabout/ Howard
Beach/ that the Lord God Almighty/ done sent
his children a message/ yes/ Jesus/ lookin
now/ for an eye for an eye/ & a tooth for a tooth/
best don't let no guinea/ let his mouth be loose/
                        hush now don't explain

i caught the Lady/ in my man's eyes
heard her tossin in his torment/ i heard Billie
Holiday in his touch/ whenever we thought
of the boy we loved so much.
                        hush now don't explain

give me an ax/ give me a machete/
get me a 9-millimeter machine gun &
just look at me/ til i see/
i say/ who/ i heard in yo eyes/
i say/ i heard Charles Mingus/
in his eyes.

174

open up/ this is the police

Open up this is the police
Open up/ you hear.

mira/ mira/ negra la policía viene
toma la coca/ toma la coca/ ahorita Inez
toma la coca/ la policia viene/

now/ heah i am 8 months gone/ 8 months
pregnant/ & i gonna swallow a ounce
of cocaine/ cuz he say . . .

mira/ mira/ toma la coca
mira/ mira/ toma la coca

. . . cuz i'm afraid/ man/ &
we'll all be separated/ i'll go to
the joint/ & there'll be some goddamned
foster parents/ & the social workers & the lawyers &
the judge/ & the AFDC & the child welfare
department/
& i'll go back to Aguas Buenas/ & they'll all say
shit/ wazn't nothin to him/ *maricon*
muy mala gente

mira/ mira/ toma la coca

& then/ maybe i'll have me a heart attack/ &
the medical examiner/ he say/ the baby
done had a heart attack/ too/ & now aint
nobody/ *ningún/* goin nowhere/ but to the chair
cuz the only right to life/ i had
i done killt/ man . . .

Mira/ mira/ toma la coca
Mira/ mira/ toma la coca

cuz my body/ is a a livin tomb/ man
a death threat/ ya get/ whatta mean?

mira/ mira/ toma la coca
mira/ mira/ toma la coca
mira/ mira/ toma la coca

                    Git down on the floor/ niggah/ face
                    down/ on the floor/
niggah. . . . . . .
        sing me a reggae dirge/ i wanna
        hear/ oh/ sing me now
"i am what i am   i am   i am   i am"/ cuz
i & i/ gonna shoot Peter Tosh tonight/
yeah/ i & i/ gonna cut the light/ right outta his
sight/ tonight/ sing/ me/ now
'i am what i am   i am   i am   i am'
                Down on the floor/
niggah/ face down on the floor/
           sing me
           a
           last
           breath
           reggae/
                niggah
hey/ Peter
sing me/
        a liberation song/

mira/ mira/ toma la coca
mira/ mira/ toma la coca

down on the floor/ face down/ on the floor

> how you like silence/ bro'dah
> how you like/ yo brains blowed out/
> ras' man/ speak to me/

speak up/ niggah

> . . . he didn't mean/ for me to die/ &
> *pequeñita esmerelda/* that waz gonna
> be her name/ Esmerelda/ if she was
> a girl
> but/ she waz a girl/ she waz a girl/
> & she dead cuz . . .

mira/ mira/ toma la coca
mira/ mira/ toma la coca

down on the floor/
face down/ on the floor/
> . . . that waz my *novio*
> that waz my child

> *"there'll be a burnin & a lootin tonight*
> *there'll be a burnin & a lootin tonight"*

he kept/ sayin/ *negra/ te amo/ escúcheme/*
negrita linda/ inez/ oígame/ te amo/ dime/
dime/ que/ la niña viva/ la niña viva
dígame/ una palabra/
> *como amor/*
> *como siempre/*

mira/ mira/ toma la coca
mira/ mira/ toma la coca

down/ on the floor
face down/ on the floor/

>in the womb/ in the dark/ we see so
>little/ we don't know our way round/
>ya see/ but Esmereldita floats cherubic/
>yeah/ in placenta waters/ streams of
>tears
>& *plenas*/ in the Bronx/ say/ Hoboken/
>Esmereldita/ *saba los ritmos* of the
>*bata y la pachanga*/ but i never saw/
>her eyes
>her eyes/ cuz i never saw her/ eyes
>you'll never see/ her eyes/ we don't
>know what she thinks/ bout the music
>in our blood/ i know/ i hear Arsenio
>Rodriquez in her eyes/ reachin
>desperate fingers/ beggin for life/
>pluck-by-pluck/ while young girls'
>bodies' slide in a hell/ that's no longer
>underground

where Peter Tosh's
head & tongue
are no more/ than
bloody spots/
somewhere/ in Jamaica

>i know/ i hear Arsenio Rodriquez
>in her eyes/

Glossary

A.I.R.—New Black Music Trio composed of Henry Threadgill (reeds), Fred Hopkins (bass), and the late Steve McCall (percussion).

Eric Dolphy—virtuoso reed man from Los Angeles whose clarity and lyricism created new attitudes towards the flute and bass clarinet in music. He died in the mid-sixties while touring Europe. See *Out to Lunch* & *Last Date*.

Charles Mingus—African-American jazz bassist and composer. See *Theme for Lester Young* & *Eat That Chicken Pie*.

Peter Tosh—guitarist, singer; and composer with reggae artist Bob Marley and the original Wailers. He was gunned down in his home in Jamaica by political marauders.

Arsenio Rodriguez—blind, black Cuban composer and cuatro player of signal importance to the development of contemporary salsa as presently understood. See *Routes to Rhythm: Chano Pozo to Ruben Blades*.

Printed in the United Kingdom
by Lightning Source UK Ltd.
135786UK00001B/18/A